Praise for
Who's In Charge of You?

"Steve has hit a homerun and uniquely touches all
the bases as he articulates his message of how to be
successful and live an amazing life."

– Dabo Swinney, Head Coach, Clemson University Football

"A success manual for the 21st century by
a modern day Dale Carnegie."

– Dave Wyman, Spiro Institute for Entrepreneurship, Clemson University

"A compelling read about how to live life to the fullest. Steve has
laid out a common-sense roadmap for life that, if followed,
will allow you to go on the offense and stay there."

– U.S. Senator Lindsey Graham

"… your message is powerful and one that my generation
should tune into if they want to be successful in business."

– Porter Fraser, college student

"Steve's message is pointed, powerful, insightful...over-invest
in activities that offer a lifetime payoff."

– Will Marre, Co-founder, Covey Leadership Center

"Steve wants you to live an amazing life, and his book
gives you the tools to do just that. His chapter on listening
is worth the price of admission."

– Neil Senturia, *I'm There For You Baby, The Entrepreneur's
Guide To The Galaxy*

"I walked away from the interview thinking to myself 'Wow, this really went well!' And your advice paid off."

– Steve Santaniello, college student

"A pity I didn't have such a wonderful tool in my formative years. Steve, where were you when I needed such guidance?"

– Betsy Byars, Newbery Medal and National Book award-winning author

---

"*Who's In Charge of You?* takes the reader on an enticing journey that is the odyssey of Steve's life, with the brilliant application of principles to empower us in both our personal and professional relationships."

– Doug Grant, CDR USN Retired - F/A-18 fighter pilot

"I really began to realize that I have control over my life, and I have the power to change the things that 'suck'."

– Sidney Ann Fowler, college student

"...brute honesty...not sugar-coated."

– John McKinley, college student

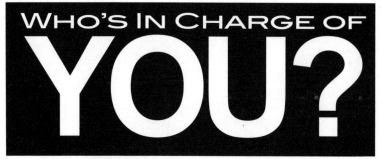

ANSWER THAT AND CHANGE
EVERYTHING

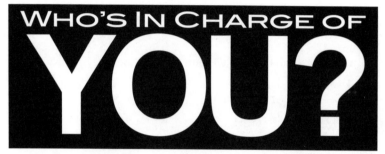

WHO'S IN CHARGE OF

YOU?

ANSWER THAT AND CHANGE
EVERYTHING

STEVE EDWARDS

Two Harbors Press
212 3rd Avenue North, Suite 290
Minneapolis, MN 55401
612.455.2293
www.TwoHarborsPress.com

ISBN-13: 978-1-936401-43-7
LCCN: 2011922340

Distributed by Itasca Books

Printed in the United States of America

DEDICATION

To Mom and Dad…you have always been a shining example of what happens when you invest hard work, integrity, patience and a lot of love into a family. We all know I tested the "patience" part more than once! Regardless, I am blessed to have you as parents and have grown from your leadership and mentoring. I'm thrilled to now pass many of these lessons on to my family and others.

To "Team Edwards"…my incredible wife and kids who stand by me in everything I do. They are the purest example of what love, happiness and family could ever be.

To my brother who stands shoulder to shoulder with me through thick and thin.

To everyone who is committed to leaving the bland world of average behind and start unlocking the doors to an amazing life!

CONTENTS

PREFACE

My childhood was much like that of an army brat...constantly moving from place to place. The difference was my folks weren't in the military; they were working to succeed in the newspaper business. My folks had a passion early in life to be their own boss and someday acquire their own newspaper. The problem was it required my father to start at the bottom rung of the ladder as district manager for a circulation department.

Knowing my parents, it's no surprise they had their eyes on the prize and were willing to do whatever it took to excel in the newspaper world. Even though we were young, my brother and I knew we had to do whatever we could to help out because it didn't take much math to know we were barely making it financially.

As it turns out, it was an amazing journey that I wouldn't trade for anything. Through the struggles, we were learning real life lessons that would carry through our entire lives.

Those lessons started young. In the old days of newspaper, the layout person would literally apply a thin film of hot wax to the back of the paper so it would stick to the layout sheet. The annoying part was that all that waxed scrap paper fell to the floor and was repeatedly stepped on all week long, virtually welding it to the wooden floor. My brother and I had to come in every weekend, get down on our hands and knees with putty knives and spend hours scraping all the wax paper off the floors. It wasn't much fun for an eight year old, but certainly necessary. We knew that if we were going to succeed as a business and as a family, everyone had to do their part.

One of the more amazing stories my folks tell is when we were living in Colorado. We were finally able to scrape up enough money to start our own tiny newspaper to compete against the much bigger newspaper in town. My folks still marvel about how we were literally one issue away from going out of business when the owner from the competing paper came in and offered to buy us out. If that hadn't happened, our company would have never survived.

We made our fifth move to Iowa when I was in seventh grade because we finally had our first chance to own a fairly good sized newspaper. Because we were still struggling financially, my mother took charge of running the paper while my father continued running newspapers for other companies.

While growing our company during the next 15 years in Iowa, I was afforded the opportunity (I'm not sure I called it opportunity back then) to be exposed to things kids today never experience. I delivered thousands of papers, sold advertising, wrote news stories, ran presses. You name it, I did it. And you know what...it was great!

No one in my family was ever afraid of work, regardless of the time or sacrifice required. Yet, through all the long hours, my folks never neglected their responsibility as parents. I honestly don't have any memories of ever having a babysitter. I still don't know how they managed to never miss one of our sports events...and there were hundreds!

I firmly believe it was what I learned during these times that prepared me to write this book, as well as share the key factors to creating amazing success with thousands of others in my speaking world. In a sense, I'm a lucky kid. I had parents who took risks and refused to accept anything but first place. Much of this rubbed off on my brother and me, which allowed us to build a successful, family owned company none of us could have dreamed of years ago.

Today I'm fortunate to travel and share my message about personal performance, taking charge of your life and living it to the fullest. Most people seem to want to live an amazing life but don't have the roadmap to get there. I hope my message lays a course for you to travel and gives you the necessary motivation to go out and live the amazing life you deserve!

INTRODUCTION

Looking down the barrel of a loaded gun is a bad time to come to the realization that your people skills need some work. Unfortunately, this is exactly where I found myself early in my business career. Just when I thought I had the world by the tail, along came a 70-year old lady packing a pistol and a really bad attitude. Believing I was trespassing, she decided the situation could be quickly and easily resolved by the use of lethal force. (See Chapter 4 for the rest of the story.)

It's remarkable how fast one's viewpoint can change with the right motivation. Looking back at that circumstance, it becomes very clear there are critical factors that impact virtually everything in and around your life — good and bad. The trick lies in recognizing these factors and utilizing some easy tips that can literally define whether the outcome of many of life's situations will be ordinary or simply amazing.

The good news is that dodging the metaphorical bullet is easier than you realize. Although there are hundreds of well-written books offering advice on how to find an amazing and successful life, I believe many authors lose sight of the fact that people trying to get their first taste of *amazing* need things kept simple. These books often (if you finish them) lead you to believe that in order to lead an incredible life, you must follow an endless list of processes. The problem is that for the average person, this mandatory list of things can easily become overwhelming and sometimes even demoralizing.

So here's the deal. I've written this book with the mindset of keeping things simple, giving you the short road to *amazing* if you will. I realize that most people *want* to be successful and do extraordinary things but are just too busy trying to work and raise families. Finding time to sit down for hours and read a thick book about making your life better just isn't realistic. *We need it quick and we need it now.* This book is written with you in mind. It's a book that doesn't mince words and doesn't waste your time. I've whittled what I believe to be the critical aspects of success down to three parts. I'm convinced these factors will have a tremendous impact on how amazing your life will turn out. They have mine. I guarantee whatever your focus — be it business, family or friends — these factors will come into play. Because of this I have set out to give it to you straight, no fluff...just straight talk about how your choices really can make or break you in life.

I find it disturbing that we live in a world where amazing is all around us, yet I see many people choosing to settle into a life that they believe is all they were destined to have. Of course, many of these people *want* to have a better life and spend many wasted hours dreaming about getting out of their rut. But, like a ship lost at sea, their hope for something better soon fades and the day-to-day routine permeates back into their lives. Before they know it, life has passed them by and the "Shoulda, Woulda, Coulda" club grows by yet another member.

I decided long ago that I wouldn't let myself go down this path (although it is definitely the path of least resistance). Instead, I have worked diligently to do some critical things that kept me on the path, which has led to professional and personal success. These choices and actions have led to some wondrous adventures, a successful business and a lot of pure quality time with my family and friends. However, when people hear about some of the *amazing* things I have done or people I know, I am often met with a puzzled look. They don't seem to understand how I managed to put myself in a position to take advantage of the unique opportunities that seem to magically come my way. But when you look back at the past 25 years of my business and personal life, you start to see many of the principles I've applied that have lead to this outcome.

Here's what no one ever tells you — with the right roadmap,

it's really not that hard to achieve. I want to show you that by taking action and making adjustments in yourself, your friends and how you work in business, you can open the door to a whole new world (and a lot of fun) that you never knew existed. You will see that all of these areas are intertwined, and by working in harmony, they create incredible results. I promise you this. By taking a little time to read this book and apply these principles somewhere in your life — whether it's your relationship with your kids, spouse, boss, friends or career — things will change for the better. Much better!

Finally, we are only here on earth for a specific amount of time. It would be a lot easier if we knew when the big buzzer in life was going to go off, but we all know that's not how it works. I know when my buzzer sounds, I want to leave knowing I've lived my life to the fullest and left a positive mark on my family and friends. So quit saying, "I'll do that when I retire" or "Maybe next time" and take a cue from Nike and..."Just Do It!"

Let's get started.

PART I

It Starts With
YOU!

❝ You can't fix stupid. ❞

{Another Steve-ism}

CHAPTER 1

Who's In Charge Of You?

Ask yourself this simple question, "Is my life where I imagined it would be?" Now, think about your answer. Interesting, isn't it? We all go through life at a million miles an hour but hardly ever stop long enough to ask ourselves if this is where we really thought we'd be at this point in life. Although many of us *want* to feel like we are living to the fullest, for many people, that isn't the case. I have found that when things are going bad, people tend to assume that it's just their destiny to live in a rut. Often times, they attempt to push the unhappiness aside by trying to run away from it. People run in a variety of ways — shopping, drinking, traveling, etc. This solution always ends up being short term because, much like pulling a weed without the roots, the problem always rears its ugly head again.

If your life sucks...then YOU SUCK!

Let's start with a quote from Larry Winget, one of my favorite authors. "If your life sucks...then YOU SUCK!" I know that's harsh, but I think it's time someone stopped sugarcoating it and explained it to you in very clear terms. As tough as this is to come to grips with, if you positively embrace the fact that whatever is going on in your life, both good and bad, is directly because YOU made it that way, unbelievable change can begin to occur. I know, I know. You're saying, "Now wait, you don't understand, I'm in this lousy position because of (insert excuse here)."

Let me help you break this down into very simple terms with

yet another question. Who's in charge of you? Although the answer seems obvious, you would be surprised how many people struggle with this. Our society is changing into one where taking responsibility for your own actions seems foreign. All we seem to hear about is how this problem was caused by *those people* or *that group* or by anything but the real person who made the mistake. When is the last time you heard someone say, "Yep, that was me...I screwed it up!" The most visible example of this is politicians. But it's not only the politicians. It's business people, teachers, parents, athletes — most anyone and everyone — because we all make mistakes. We all try to shift the blame when failure happens and conversely, try to grab the credit for the successes. It's a natural human response. Now I could write an entire book about how people place blame anywhere but on themselves, but this book is about you. So let's take a look at a few areas of your life that might need some review.

A life filled with joy and happiness isn't as difficult as many make it out to be. The kind of life you lead, both positive and negative, really comes down to the kind of decisions you make... and not just the big important decisions. Many of the decisions are the small, mundane choices you make everyday that drive your success and happiness...or lack of it.

I have said many times that if you dissect the lives of successful people it quickly becomes evident that every one of them has been successful because they made a series of good decisions throughout their life. Now this isn't to say they haven't screwed up a time or two. It just means the good decisions far outweigh the negative ones. They also realized when they started making poor decisions they didn't allow it to grow to the point of no return. Instead, they changed it and started making positive ones again. The reverse holds true for people having difficulties in life.

Simple enough, right? Maybe, maybe not. But coming to grips with the realization that virtually *everything* in your life is a direct

CHAPTER 2

Where's The Bar?

Have you ever been to an apple orchard? It only takes a moment to recognize there are three very different qualities of apples on each tree. First, there are the ones that fell off the tree and are rotting on the ground. Next are the ones hanging on the low branches that have been picked over so many times that it's difficult to find one that really suits your desire. Finally, there are the apples at the top of the tree just out of reach. These apples all look nearly perfect and the likelihood of a delicious apple is much greater up high. The problem is that it takes a lot more effort to reach them.

Although this metaphor is fairly obvious, stop and ask yourself which apple you are eating. Here's the good news — just taking the time to read this book shows that you want the best fruit in your life.

As you well know, the rotten fruit on the ground is the easiest to find and fill your stomach, but it's not fun to eat and really doesn't taste that great. Most people know to avoid this fruit.

The low hanging fruit is also pretty easy to reach, but you can spend hours trying to find one good apple. The good ones have been so picked over, that the results of your search are disappointing.

The fruit at the top of the tree is the most fulfilling and best of all — there aren't that many people up there trying to eat it. Although reaching it takes planning and effort, the first sweet, juicy bite reminds you that it was worth it.

The sad reality is most people go through their entire life eating rotten apples or settling for second-rate, low-hanging fruit rather than going for the best fruit at the top of the tree. Let's talk about why.

Most people have their bar set way too low.

Everyone has certain desires and hopes for what kind of life they want to live. I call this "Setting the Bar." I believe that where you set your personal bar usually determines how successful or amazing your life is. This I can guarantee you — most people have their bar set way too low because they simply don't think they are capable of achieving the success required at a higher level.

There are only three reasons for not raising your bar: 1) you don't have the knowledge, 2) you don't think you deserve any better or worse, or 3) you have no desire to make an effort.

No one can provide you with desire, but sometimes some knowledge and confidence can go a long way in raising the bar. Unfortunately, we live in a society where it is not only commonplace but acceptable to place responsibility for our problems on the actions of others. This makes failures in your life easier to digest because you can say it wasn't your fault. Many times this attitude becomes engrained at an early age due to poor parenting, schooling and a variety of other factors. From there it gets comfortable and quietly develops into full-blown laziness over the years. (To make matters worse, our school systems appear to foster this poor attitude instead of creating an environment of responsibility for one's own actions early in life. But this is a topic for another book.)

There are some places that simply refuse to allow this behavior to develop. Better yet, they stop it at an early age. My son goes to a school that is known to be academically challenging, as well as a loving environment. One night, my wife and I were at a meeting, and some of the parents were questioning the principal about why the school was so demanding on the kids and why there was so much homework. His answer spoke volumes. He simply said that they set the bar to a very high level and *then they never move it.* Period! He went on to say it is amazing to watch how quickly the kids adapt and find ways to get over it when they realize the bar isn't going to move. He assured us that by the end of the year, all of our kids would be stronger, smarter and more responsible than they (or we) ever thought possible. As it turns out, he was right, but we had some doubts at first. Early in the year, my son came home and told me he got in trouble for walking into class three seconds late (literally three seconds) and didn't think it was fair. I could tell he felt sure that I would come to his rescue. Instead, I decided to turn it into a teaching moment, as well as a lifelong lesson. I explained to him that three seconds, three minutes, whatever, late is late.

Although this is a minor thing in middle school, it will apply throughout his entire life. It is also an excellent example of unwillingness to move the bar. Needless to say, after the teacher explained to him the ramifications of his actions, he's never been late again. After a year of school and numerous teaching moments from both us as parents as well as from the teachers, I have seen him show incredible growth in his ability to take responsibility for his successes and failures throughout all areas of his life. On top of that, he really enjoys the school.

One last example that really brings home the point came to me through an experience with the military. Whether you know it or not, 18-year olds are protecting you and this country. We all know about the brave soldiers fighting overseas who put their lives on the line every day. However, in this example, I'm talking about young kids right here in the United States. I visited a secure military location that, through extremely high tech equipment, monitors all of our nation's borders for any sign of hostility over the ground, through the air or from space. If America were to have a hostile action against it, these folks were going to see it first and sound the alarms. I was somewhat surprised when I walked in a darkened room where no one was talking, just working multiple monitors and screens with expert precision. I was so impressed by these 18-year olds I asked the commanding officer how they managed to instill such responsibility in these young kids. He said that when you expect a certain degree of performance (very high in this case) many people are capable of reaching it. He went on to say, "The biggest problem is that most people don't hold kids accountable like the military does and the result is obvious all around us."

Both my son's school and the Army high-tech command have set the bar high and kept it there. The young people who meet that challenge enjoy the success and the good apples that reaching this height provides.

So before you continue reading, stop and take a minute to consider this. Where you set the bar has an impact on EVERYTHING in your life. I don't care what it is — your career, family, friends, even your spouse. Set the bar too low and *everything* suffers for it. But you suffer the most.

THINGS TO REMEMBER

TWO
Reach For The Best Apples High On The Tree

THREE
Raise The Bar In Your Life

CHAPTER 3

Idiot Friends

I firmly believe that if you hang around idiots you will become one — no exceptions. There are people in your life who make you a better person and then there are ones who strive to bring you down to their level of misery. The problem is most of us don't take the time to figure out who is who.

I am convinced that for someone to grow as an individual, that person must associate with people who have a desire to grow and become a better person as well. Sounds obvious, right? It's not, mainly because most people never take the time to stop and figure it out. I challenge you to take a minute and write down your top five friends. By the way, if you can't write down five friends in less than a minute then they really aren't your friends anyway. Now sit back and take a serious look at the list, not a cursory look, but a serious look. If it helps, write down the positive and negative traits each person has. Regardless of how you analyze the list, I'm sure you will have at least one person in your life that does absolutely nothing to make you better, and possibly even more than one.

Now let me be clear here. I'm not talking about someone who has a job that is below the level you are, or who doesn't have the same financial status as you. I'm talking about character. Which one of your friends exhibits traits that you hope to gain and grow from and which ones don't? The friends on the idiot list are usually selfish and find great joy in sharing negative gossip about others. They will do everything in their power to make you feel that lack of success is just fine because that's where they are, soaking in a life of mediocrity. In fact, that's where most people are — sitting around complaining about their lack of good fortune and how nothing seems to go their way, yet doing nothing at all to change their situation. Sound like someone you know? Change it! Remove the negative influences and seek out new, more positive people.

I have also found that the more successful you become in your life, and the more you grow as an individual, the more the need to reevaluate your friends becomes evident. It is imperative that you make sure the people you are associating with not only bring character to the table, but also help you see the world from a bigger stage. I have friends who earn less money than I do, and friends who have enough money for several lifetimes. What brings us together are similarities in our beliefs, ethics and morals — not our income levels.

One of these people is my friend Peter. Not only is Peter a great guy, but he has traveled the world many times over and has developed some of the neatest pieces of real estate in the country. On top of that, he is currently developing his own island in the Caribbean. I'm not talking part of an island — I'm talking the whole enchilada. That's amazing! In his career, he has dealt with some of the richest people in the world, but because he is such a down-to-earth kind of guy, you would never know it... that's what makes it great to call him a friend. He pushes me to new heights in my thinking and is always willing to help me at a moment's notice.

Another person worth mentioning is my friend Blake. A few years back, he helped me coach our kids' baseball team. Our team typically played their games at five o'clock in the afternoon. Because his job called for him to travel quite a bit, it wasn't unusual for him to call and say that although he was five hours away, he would still be there in time to help coach the game. Here's the kicker — because he wasn't finished working in that particular town, he would get up at four o'clock the next morning so he could drive back down there for another workday. Overall, he would drive ten hours just so he could be part of his kid's one-hour game. Even though he did this multiple times throughout the season, he never told anyone but me he was doing it. Do you know any dads that would do that for their kids? I don't. I'm not even sure I would. That's why we are such good friends. He is a constant reminder of what generosity, family first and a positive outlook can do for someone.

So think about your friends and ask how many of them really provide examples in the way they live their life that makes you better? If you can't find any, this should be your first red flag that maybe it's time for some change.

I was taught at an early age to give without expecting anything in return, to give more than you receive and to give regardless of the time, money or sacrifice required. What gets tiring is when I give and give and give, and then when I need something from a friend I've helped they can't or won't do it. Because of this, I haven't stopped giving, but I have learned to ask myself this simple question before I go to my usual lengths of helping someone. "Would they do it for me if the situation was reversed?" It's sad, but many times the answer is "no." As hard as it is for me, I will either turn them down or not do all I could have done to help them out. I also use this as a quick self test of whether or not these are really the people I want in my close circle of friends.

On the flip side, I have about four people on my anything list. This is a group of friends, outside of my family, who are simply as good as it gets. I know I would help them with anything they needed 24/7 because they would do the same for me. Now that's something special. Can you name anyone who would do that for you?

I don't think I'm a materialistic person, but I still have a natural desire to own unique things. It's not always an expensive thing, just different. The problem is many people don't like anyone who is different from them. They want everyone to live the same ordinary life that they are living, and this can have an unexpected impact. This impact can take the shape of encouragement or jealousy, depending on your friends.

Consider this — I own and fly an airplane. Now, if you want to find out about your friends, just go buy something as unique as an airplane. I have owned three airplanes so far and each time I got one there has only been one pilot, my buddy Dwaine who lives 500 miles away, who calls me every time and tells me how happy he is for me. We both know he would kill to own a plane like mine and realizes a purchase like that doesn't come easy. Regardless, he invites me to tell him all about the new plane and all the new avionics. That's character!

On the flip side, I've never had a fellow pilot at my own airport express any sense of happiness — quite the opposite has occurred. Growing up, my mother told us endlessly that, "Most people are not happy for your success." Although I have found that to be incredibly true, I think it comes with one variable. I find that *successful* people are indeed happy for your success, mainly because they understand it's the natural by-product of hard work and dedication.

....
If you hang around idiots you become one — guaranteed!
....

Here's one last story to bring this point home. Years ago, I made friends with a guy we will call Jeff. I was single then and had a lot of free time to hang out at Jeff's house with his wife and kids. However, after about six months I discovered a problem — Jeff was an idiot. He usually saw the negative in everything and enjoyed exploiting peoples' misfortunes. Worst of all, he would constantly have a smart mouth toward people and usually answered his wife (who was an incredibly wonderful person) with a put-down. At first, it seemed like he was just having fun, but after a while I realized that what seemed funny was actually a mean spirited, selfish, insecure guy talking. What really woke me up was when I started hearing myself saying some of the same smart aleck put-downs toward people. In essence, I was becoming like him. Fortunately, I recognized my poor behavior early and decided that wasn't how I wanted to live my life. It also dawned on me if I continued hanging out with him I was never going to change. Our friendship soon faded as I made new friends who exemplified the type of attitude I wanted to personify. That was over 15 years ago and from what I've heard, his life hasn't gotten any better. I bet he's still wondering why.

If you hang around idiots, you become one — guaranteed! Fortunately, the opposite of this is also true. Hanging around with people who are better than you makes you better.

THINGS TO REMEMBER

FOUR
Hang Around With Friends Who Make You Better

CHAPTER 4

Woulda Coulda Shoulda, DID

Which one are you? My family has this cartoon hanging on most of the bathroom mirrors in our house. I find this cartoon, as silly as it is, to be my motto in life. I don't have time to be in second place; I want to live life to the fullest and do things. We live in a world of people who always *want* to do something, or *will* someday but somehow they never actually do it. I think Nike hit the nail on the head with the slogan "Just Do It." That speaks volumes to me. I find it aggravating when I'm hanging around people who are the "Woulda, Coulda, Shoulda" types. It is a complete waste of my time to hear wishful stories. If you really want to do something then you will find a way to get it done. Problem is, most people don't really want it bad enough.

Please don't give me excuses like, "I don't have the time" or

"If I had more money, I would." Quit fooling yourself! You just don't want it bad enough...period. I marvel at how fat people can find time to eat and watch five hours of TV a night, but somehow never find time to workout. I wonder how many fat people watch "Biggest Loser" without using it as motivation to get off the couch and lose some weight.

You would be surprised if you took the time to find a few things in your life that you've always wanted to do and then did the unthinkable — you just did them! Most of the time, the barrier is not financial — it's commitment on your part. I've always wanted to learn how to play guitar, but I didn't want to spend the time or money paying for lessons. What did I do? I found a handy little tutorial on my Mac computer that teaches me via video, step by step, how to play. Don't have a Mac? How about YouTube? I could go on and on. The point is that if you truly want to do something, you will find a way to accomplish it.

Ask yourself this. What is something you would do if you knew you couldn't fail? Think about that for a while. Find a reason to want it so bad that it consumes your thoughts and then just go for it! Believe me, if you don't grab the prize someone else will. Why not you? Quit talking about it and start taking steps toward accomplishing it. I don't care if it's that amazing vacation you've always dreamed of, asking that girl/guy out for coffee, or finding a job that makes you jump out of bed in the morning — find it and amazing things start to occur!

Being a person in the "DID" category will often show leadership in you that you never knew you had. About a year ago, I was in bed watching a late night infomercial. It showed me how I can do a workout program at home called P90X and go from having flabby muscles to being ripped in 90 days. I spent quite a while studying the commercial, made sure they had a money back guarantee, and I bought the program. Then I did what most people don't do and made a conscious decision to complete the 90 days NO MATTER WHAT.

Let me tell you, getting ripped in 90 days doesn't come easy. After the first couple of days I hurt in places I didn't know existed. I told my wife that because of the pain, 85% of the people who start this program quit. My kids were watching me work out in front of the TV every day, and I wasn't about to let some short-term pain stop me, or worse, show my kids firsthand what a quitter looked like. Guess what? Ninety days later I was ripped (for me anyway) and had a lot of people asking me what I did to look so good. I explained the program to them and now I can name over a dozen people who do the same workout because I did it. That's leadership in my book! Would it have been easier to roll over in bed, turn the TV off and go to sleep? Absolutely! But I didn't and my life got better because of it. I'm sure watching me count down from 90 days and seeing the results made an impact on my kids as well. Imagine if I had quit? It would have the same impact with a completely different result.

You just don't want it bad enough ... period.

I believe this trait is one of the primary things required in a person in order to experience a richer life. You must be someone who likes to do things — not talk about them — do them! If you want to talk about it, fine; just don't expect great things in your future. I strive to be the guy who gets things done. My friends are well aware of this fact. They know that once I say I'm going to do something, it's as good as done. I simply don't allow myself to talk about things without taking some action on it.

I'd love to write another book someday called Dead in 30 Days because I often wonder what people would do differently in their life if they knew they had 30 days before it was game over. Think about that for a while. If you knew the clock had just started, what would you do differently? I bet you wouldn't just sit back and talk about doing things anymore. I'm amazed how people assume they have a long time to live (is that guaranteed somewhere?). Assuming they have plenty of time, they often say something like, "I'll get to it later." I bet you know someone who either had their life cut short due to an illness or accident, or worked hard their whole career waiting to enjoy retirement only to die a short time after. I agree you can't do it all right now, but you sure can at least have a plan to get started because you never know when you're going to kick the oxygen habit like I almost did early in my career.

In the early 90's I was working long hours as the publisher of a newspaper. Next to our building was a 70-year old lady operating a consignment shop. Although we both had parking lots for our businesses, there were six public parking spaces along the street that were shared because we were neighboring businesses. She always took it personally when one of our customers parked in one of the six spaces (remember this was public parking) and would call our office endlessly until the offending car was moved. She would even start calling when a delivery truck would stop there for five minutes.

Finally, the day came when I was going to add on to our existing building. The good news was the construction included a brand new parking lot, which would forever eliminate our customers from parking in her spots. The bad news was during construction we were going to have to use the spaces quite frequently because our old parking lot was getting torn up to make room for the expansion. I went over to her business to explain the good and bad news to her. Unfortunately, she saw it as bad and worse news. After twenty minutes of going back and forth I got fed up and said, "They're public spaces and there's nothing you can do to stop us from being there." That was a big mistake. As I turned to go out the door, she pulled a pistol from her desk and, with a remarkably steady hand, pointed it at my chest. I was only about ten feet away and I knew she couldn't miss. Needless to say, I immediately deemed ALL the spaces to be hers forever! After a few long minutes of emphasizing that we would never, ever park there again, I eased myself out the door and into safety.

The point is, you never know when your last day will be. So ask yourself this, if you died at the end of the month, would you have done all you hoped? I doubt it. Try turning the TV and electronics off for a night and actually *doing* something. Start small and work up from there. But whatever you do, stop being the "Coulda Woulda Shoulda" person and start being the person who "DID" it.

THINGS TO REMEMBER

FIVE
You've Gotta Want It

CHAPTER 5

I Dare You

You want to get my attention? Just say you will "try" — or worse — tell me you "can't" accomplish something. I will immediately tell you that you are full of crap! Those two words are the most irritating and, at the same time, inspirational words that could ever be spoken to me. First, anyone who tells you they will try to do something is really telling you they aren't going to do it. Either you are or you aren't — there isn't any middle ground. I'm fine if you say you are going to do your best but don't you dare say you're going to try. Think about it. How would you feel if you got on a commercial airliner and the captain came on and said, "Welcome aboard ladies and gentlemen. This is your captain speaking, and I'm going to *try* to fly us to our destination." I bet most people would go running off the plane. Nothing portrays lack of confidence or lack of effort more than saying, "I'll try." If you start listening for those words, you will be surprised how often you and others say them.

······························
No one but me has the right to tell me I can't accomplish something.
······························

That's the irritating part — the inspirational part is when someone says "Can't." I admit that saying "can't" is better than saying "try." At least I know which side of the fence you're on, but when you tell me that I can't do something, I get inspired! I will do everything short of killing myself trying to prove you wrong! No one but me has the right to tell me I can't accomplish something. The same should apply to you. Don't let people make you believe you can't do something.

Back in my college days, I decided to run a marathon. I'm a fairly big guy at 6'3" and about 215 pounds. You really don't see guys my size running marathons, especially back in the eighties. The beating your body takes is compounded by your size. This is why all those stringy little 120 pounders always win. Now keep in mind that before this started, I had battled asthma and was never really able to run more than three miles or so because I would just about stop breathing. So here I am one day in my college dorm room, and God only knows what possessed me to decide to train and run a marathon. I probably thought it would be another unique thing most people never accomplish. I needed more information, so I went out and bought some books on how to train for a marathon and read them with great interest. The books said if you were dedicated and ran short runs that progressively got longer, in six to twelve months you would be able to complete a 26.2 mile race. Sound familiar? I bet you could apply that theory to a lot more things in life than just a marathon.

Early in my training I had every reason to quit. The muscle pain I experienced was awful, and worst of all, my asthma was brutal. At that time, I didn't know about or use an asthma inhaler which immediately remedies the effects of asthma, so all I could do was run through the misery. (Side note here, for all of you that are lucky enough not to have asthma, here is what it feels like: go out and run for about a mile at a good pace and then plug your nose and insert a straw between your lips and clench down on it. Continue running, but now only breathe through the straw for the next three miles. As hard as it becomes to breathe, you can't unplug your nose or take the straw out — that's what asthma feels like.)

One day, I was walking through one of my college hallways,

and I came upon a guy who asked me what I'd been up to. I told him I was training for a marathon, and without hesitation, he uttered those memorable words, "You can't run a marathon. You're too big." I just smiled and thought to myself that thanks to him, nothing in the world would stop me. Part of me wanted to thank him and part of me wanted to kill him. Regardless, it gave me all the motivation I needed. I trained most days at 5:30 a.m. before class (remember you find the time if you want it bad enough) and continued religiously six days a week for eight straight months. My asthma was bad during many runs, but I kept pressing on with what little air I could garner. Afterwards, it would often take me over half an hour to change clothes because it took all my effort just to breathe.

My college was in Iowa, and I trained through three seasons — winter being the worst. I ran in every kind of weather imaginable. My worst experience was running in forty below wind chill. During that run, my sweat was freezing inside of my clothes to the point where I actually looked like I was going in slow motion because my clothes had virtually frozen up. Regardless, I never missed a single day of training.

Eight months and thirty-five pounds lighter, I was ready to run a marathon. A few weeks before the race, I decided that I wouldn't stop during the entire 26.2 miles. I don't know why I thought it was important not to walk or rest, maybe it was my way of saying absolutely nothing would stop me. Three hours and forty-two minutes later, I came across the finish line never having to stop. I lost eight pounds during the race, and it was brutally hard near the end but I DID it. Twenty years later, it still ranks as one of the top ten accomplishments in my life. So much for telling me, "I can't." If you want it bad enough, you CAN do anything!

What about you? Start listening for others — including yourself — to say the words "try" and "can't" and find some irritation and motivation from them. My kids even hear it now and raise an eyebrow when they hear someone say "try." I cringe on the rare occasion when they ask me if I'll do something, and I pass off the question with a quick, "Okay, I'll try." I can't help but smile when they frown and remind me that "try" doesn't cut it.

Finally, what have you done, or more importantly, what are you going to do that ranks in your top ten accomplishments? Go do something that no one can ever take away from you! If you do, I guarantee you will cherish the memory for a lifetime.

THINGS TO REMEMBER

SIX
Take The Dare and Just Do It

SEVEN
Turn I'll Try and I Can't into I WILL and I CAN

CHAPTER 6

You're A Slob

I once read "if your teenager's room is a wreck, just close the door, it's too late." Ask yourself, why do you tolerate being a slob or being around them? Slobs have a ton of excuses why their office, house, car, etc. is a disaster, but that's all they are — excuses. Being a slob in any aspect of your life tells me two things: you're lazy and you have no pride.

I have a friend who is a regional manager for one of the biggest retailers in America. He marvels over the fact that people come in for interviews looking completely pathetic. His choice of words was interesting when he told me, "When they walk into my office, I know this is the best they will ever look." He's right! Whether it's your job interview or your wedding, there are moments that show the world, "Here I am...it doesn't get any better than this!" Make sure you know when those moments are.

Here's something no one tells you — people who are working to be high achievers don't tolerate slobs. I have no desire to go to someone's house that is a wreck or to be with someone who is a slob. Most of all, I have no tolerance for someone who keeps a sloppy desk. I know, I know! Your desk is a wreck but you know where everything is and that's how you work best. I say you are not only lying to me but to yourself as well. From my experience, organized people can work circles around slobs. I see it everyday.

Fortunately, it only takes two things to fix the problem, a little time and a lot of pride. I have been in many college classrooms, and I am constantly astounded at the students' complete and utter sloppiness. Working as an "Entrepreneur in Residence" within college classrooms I have personally witnessed students giving their final presentations sporting a shirt and pants that are so wrinkled they look like they had been bundled up in a ball for the last month. I wanted to stop them before they even started and simply tell them, "You lost me at the first wrinkle and your grade will reflect it." It's hard to figure out if they don't know what an iron is, or if they are just too lazy to use it. Any guesses what their bedrooms and closets look like? How about when they show up for that important interview? Just know this, slobs are the last to get hired and the first to get fired.

························

Slobs are the last to get hired and the first to get fired.

························

My wife and I have created what we feel are some positive family habits. One thing we do is make sure our kids keep their rooms clean and their appearance neat. They know that vacuuming the house, doing the dishes or cleaning our cars are just things we do to help each other out. They have a daily chore list that helps them to remember what needs to be done. We don't give an allowance and they don't expect one. We believe that we're all part of a family, and since we share the same house, cleaning it should be a team effort. It wasn't easy at first, but now it's a habit that comes naturally to them. Don't get me wrong. Their rooms aren't immaculate, but I bet they are cleaner than most of their friends' rooms. Of course there are days their rooms have been a total wreck. When this happens, we simply ask them if they would be proud of it if we had some guests come over. They know the answer without having to give us an excuse. Instead, they just fix the problem.

So do this — look at your life and find the areas that need some cleaning up. Go find a full length mirror and use it. Take the time to get organized at home and work. You'll not only become more efficient, but much more effective in these areas of your life as well. Regardless, don't con yourself with some lame excuse justifying why you're living the life of a slob. The only person you're fooling is yourself.

THINGS TO REMEMBER

EIGHT
Clean Up Your Act

CHAPTER 7

Drive It Like You Stole It

I live close to one of BMW's manufacturing plants where many of their popular models of cars are made. Adjacent to the facility is what they call their "Performance Driving Center" where they safely show you all the attributes and handling of their various models of cars and trucks. In my opinion, "Performance Driving Center" is just BMW's code word for "our own racetrack where there's no police and speed is not an issue." My friend Doug, who oversees the racetrack, recently asked me to invite a group of business owners and leaders to come out and experience the performance facility for free. The hope was that we would all be motivated to bring our leadership teams back for future paid programs. I can't remember being more popular with my friends. I filled the twenty positions in the blink of an eye!

Driving up to the facility, my blood pressure rose (as did my testosterone level) when I saw all of BMW's high performance cars lined up waiting for us to take the wheel. Best of all, I knew the keys were just inside the door. For the BMW folks, the trick is finding a way for you to have a memorable, fun learning experience without wrecking their cars and killing yourself. After a pleasant reception, we had a short introductory meeting to better understand the rules of the race track. All of us had the same question on our mind, "How hard will they let me drive these cars?" It was then that one of the instructors stood up and said, "Drive it like you stole it." I think all twenty of us smiled and laughed at the same time.

BMW knew something we didn't. They knew that real growth in our driving skills would never happen if we didn't push the limits. With their supervision, as well as some in-depth instruction, we safely pushed ourselves and the cars further than most of us had ever dared to go. Not only was it a tremendous learning experience, it was a ton of fun. Needless to say, whenever I get together with one of those twenty guys, we always talk about what a great day that was. The point is that most of us accomplished things in a car that we had never done before because we didn't know it was possible. Most driving is spent going in straight lines and slower speeds. It's not until you push the car and yourself that you really start to appreciate the experience, as well as your ability to handle it.

Push the pedal to the floor and see what you're made of!

I hope you appreciate the metaphor here. Why do most people live their lives at a much slower pace than they are capable of going? Because it's comfortable and more importantly... it's SAFE! My philosophy is there are times you need to test yourself. Push the pedal to the floor and see what you're made of! There are many ways you can do this; maybe it's taking your family on an adventure vacation instead of the same old routine. How about doing something others would consider daring? Take a look at what your kids like to do and find an adventure that would be exciting for all of you. Doing something out of your comfort zone often times results in lifetime memories. I'm also willing to bet you'll find that you were capable of much more than you ever thought possible.

If that illustration doesn't hit home let me try this one. A while back, I listened to the State of the State address given by our Governor. After all the typical political rhetoric, he decided to end his speech on a topic far from politics. Here's what he said. "In early December, I had an amazing conversation with

Ric Elias, who found himself in seat 1A of the plane that went down in the Hudson River. The plane lifted off from LaGuardia, and a short time after takeoff the captain came on mentioning a bird strike and matter-of-factly said that they would have to head back to the airport to land. Ric's position was interesting because he sat catty-corner to the flight attendant and saw no fear in her eyes as the captain spoke. Another couple minutes go by and the captain comes back on announcing just three words, "Prepare for impact." At that point, he could see the sheer horror in the flight attendant's eyes as she knew what that meant. They were fully loaded with fuel and you don't set a jet of that size down on a street in Queens, Brooklyn or Manhattan.

"Ric did the mental calculation and figured he would be dying in about 40 to 45 seconds and his whole life went rolling by. He said even though he had previously had the natural fears of death, he was not afraid of death when it was so near. What he did think about was the time he had wasted — the time he had spent arguing about petty things, about things that didn't matter with people who did, the times he had let little things get to him. He said it was the most amazing process of letting go of all these things in those 45 seconds. In essence, he died to himself and to those previous aggravations in the short window of time that he had left on earth.

"But he didn't die, and now he compares life to playing on bonus time in a video game — he shouldn't be here, but he is, and therefore he is going to fully live each day. In profoundly positive ways, he will work to make a difference in the lives of those around him and the world at large. He will invest in things that truly matter — those things that you can't see, you can't touch, you can't feel — but are the things that will have lasting value."

Stop and think about what you are doing in your life right now that in the big scheme of things just isn't worth wasting your time on. If it were you looking out that window knowing your life was about over, what would go through your mind? Look around your life and figure out where you could be pressing the pedal down more. Remember, the older you are the less the pedal will go down. Go out and test yourself! You will see life has a lot more to offer for those who are willing to get uncomfortable and push their limits to the max. I'll also guarantee you this — pushing yourself to new limits is truly where lifetime memories are made. I've done a lot of amazing things in my life, but it's the times that I've stepped out of my comfort zone that are the most memorable.

THINGS TO REMEMBER

NINE
Test Yourself — Push The Pedal To The Floor

TEN
Live Like You Are Dying

IN A NUTSHELL
10 Ways To Take Charge Of Your Life

ONE
You Are In Charge Of You

TWO
Reach for The Best Apples High On The Tree

THREE
Raise The Bar In Your Life

FOUR
Hang Around With Friends Who Make You Better

FIVE
You've Gotta Want It

SIX
Take The Dare and Just Do It

SEVEN
Turn I'll Try and I Can't into I WILL and I CAN

EIGHT
Clean Up Your Act

NINE
Test Yourself — Push The Pedal To The Floor

TEN
Live Like You Are Dying

" **The question is the answer.** **"**

{Another Steve-ism}

Part II • It's Not About You!

CHAPTER 8

Everyone's Favorite Subject

Me, me, me — I love talking about me! I don't care where you are or who you're with, everyone's favorite subject is always the same — themselves. Most of us won't admit it of course, because that would sound too self-serving or arrogant. But, if you dig down and look, you too will agree that nothing is more enjoyable to talk about than yourself. Here's the problem! No one really wants to hear it. Why? Because it cuts into the time they have to talk about themselves.

Why is this important in the big scheme of things? Because it's one of the fundamentals to expanding your social and professional network. Remember the old saying, "It's not what you know but who you know?" I've taken it one step further: "It's not who you know. It's what you know about *who* you know that is the key. In other words, everyone has a skill, passion or story; however, most people are never asked to talk about it. The result is a wasted opportunity to learn something you most likely never knew about someone. What makes things even more difficult is that the people who are wealthy or have truly unique backgrounds are usually the hardest to get to know. Why? Not because they are working for the CIA or some other secret agency, but compared to others, they are living in what I call rare air and don't want to appear better than everyone by sharing their unique stories. These folks tend to keep their mouths shut about themselves, but here's the interesting thing. They aren't any different from anyone else; they *want* to talk about themselves but just need a good reason to do so.

It's funny how conversations can go — or don't go — as the case may be. Remember, when you're talking about people's favorite subject, they usually become instantly engaged in both you and the conversation. Many times I notice people smiling as they are telling me about themselves. However, asking questions just to suck up or schmooze doesn't work at all. What does work is pure, unadulterated curiosity. If you are genuinely curious about the other person's life stories then questions will come easily. It sounds simple but it isn't for most people. There are many reasons for this, but the main one is that most people really don't have a desire to be curious, nor do they have the ability to *listen*.

You can't learn if your lips are moving.

People forget that asking questions requires good old-fashioned listening. Remember the adage, "You can't learn if your lips are moving." Nothing says it better when it comes to networking and making new friends. Did you know that the reason most people can't remember a person's name immediately after being introduced to them is because their entire focus is getting their own name out correctly? Again, it's not just questions that are important, but the willingness to listen and the ability to ask the *right* questions about someone else. Don't worry, these skills can be easily learned, but it takes a basic understanding of why they are important to be motivated to do so.

For starters, you must realize that many people have far more interesting stories and experiences than you could ever imagine. Yes, there will be some unbelievably boring people you come across, but many times you would be shocked by what you could learn from someone who, on the outside, looks like they have little to offer. If nothing else, remember this! As enjoyable as it is to talk about yourself — haven't you heard all of your stories before? Are you really growing by sharing all of your great knowledge with others? No, of course not. Start looking at the other people around you and start deciphering what they are all about.

Let me give you an example. A couple of years ago, my wife and I were invited to a party at a friend's house in a neighboring state. Midway through the party, I was talking with a group of strangers about our common enjoyment of flying. Standing in the group was a 70-year old man named Fred. As we all shared some of our aviation stories with each other, I noticed that Fred listened intently but remained reserved throughout the entire discussion. Since I always try to include everyone in the conversation, I asked Fred if he owned an airplane. He said he did and went on to mispronounce the name of it. Now if there is one thing I really know it's airplanes. I found it surprising, to say the least, that the plane he owned was worth over three million dollars, and yet he couldn't pronounce it's name correctly. Hmmm... I asked him some more basic questions about the plane, none of which he could answer. Finally, he simply said, "All I know is that when I call for the plane to be ready, it's always there when I show up." Needless to say, he had my interest. Remarkably, the others in the discussion became bored and left to meander about the party. Not me. I was intrigued, so I continued to chat and ask questions to figure out what Fred was all about. I started by asking what he did before he retired. He answered me with a question of his own. He asked if I ever used those machines where you swipe your credit card through to make a charge at a store. I said, "Of course," and he responded with the famous words, "That was me." He went on to explain that he had sold his company a few years back and was now a venture capitalist who invested in a variety of projects.

Later that evening, Fred and I went with our wives to a concert. During an intermission, we stepped into the hallway to fetch some drinks. Because our friendship was growing over the past few hours, Fred finally let down his guard. He told me, "Steve, virtually every deal that comes through this town usually makes it to my desk." Although that was a big statement, he said it without any arrogance, just simple fact. Better yet, he extended an invitation for me to come over any time I chose to sit in with his group and listen to some deals. Did he enjoy telling me about his successes? Yes! So much so that he invited me into a group many would kill to join.

I got so much more out of learning about Fred by asking questions and listening rather than bragging about myself and my exploits. The main point of the story is this — no one in the group gave a hoot about a 70-year old quiet guy at the party. No one except me. This is one of the primary keys to networking: be curious. Did my life get better for it? Absolutely! To this day, Fred is a good friend who has introduced me to several unique investment opportunities — deals I would have never known existed if I hadn't taken the time to be curious about him. It's WHAT you know about WHO you know!

Now I'm not saying you shouldn't share *anything* about yourself. In fact, many people do have an interest in you or they wouldn't be talking to you in the first place. The key, at least in the beginning, is what I call the misdirect. This is simply answering a question in a very brief way and then asking the other person more questions. The goal is to keep the spotlight off of you and on the other person. Remember, you will not be met with resistance because you're just allowing the other person to get back to what they like the most...talking about themselves.

Periodically, my wife and I invite people we meet out to dinner in the hopes of fostering some new friendships. Many times, the people are so caught up in talking about themselves that when the dinner is over, we chuckle over the fact that they don't know anything about us other than our names. Do you ever notice that someone who can't shut up actually pushes people away from them? The worst part is they seldom realize it's happening. Admit it! Don't you hesitate to answer the phone when you see the name of a big talker on the other end? It's probably because of these people that text messaging has become such a hit. The key networking point here is this — don't invest a lot of time in people who don't show any desire to know about you.

Once you realize there are many people who have some incredibly interesting stories to tell, your learning curve will immediately start going up and your network will begin expanding. Of course, like the dinner mentioned previously, there is some culling you must do in order to find the stars in the crowd. Regardless, I urge you to re-ignite your curiosity and start asking people questions about themselves. If nothing else, make it your own private game of how little you can talk about yourself and how much you can learn from others. I guarantee you'll find that everyone has a story and most people are sincerely appreciative you asked about it.

THINGS TO REMEMBER

ONE
It's What You Know
About Who You Know

TWO
Everyone Wants To Talk About Their
Passions — Let Them

CHAPTER 9

The Question Is The Answer

So what makes someone suddenly decide to become more curious? I believe the answer is best seen when you take a look at how small steps can produce large results over time. My curiosity started developing many years ago when I was in college. I was constantly asking people I met what they did for a living. I remember my girlfriend accusing me of trying to compare myself to what they did. I, of course, laughed and reminded her that a college guy doesn't have anything to compare. I simply liked learning about things I didn't understand. Anytime I met someone who had a job doing something I didn't know about I would question them with genuine curiosity until I had at least a basic understanding of it.

....
Am I really asking the right questions?
....

Asking about someone's career or, better yet, what they like to do when they are *not* working is often the easiest way to enter into a conversation. Think about it. Most of us know very little about anything other than what *we* do on a daily basis. This makes it very difficult to find anything in common with the other party. How do you solve this? As I have said many times, "The question is the answer!"

I've discovered after 25 years of asking questions and being curious that I have "an ocean of knowledge an inch deep". Seldom does a conversation occur where I don't know at least *something* about the topic. Now I know what you're saying,

"Some people are just boring and have nothing to offer." I agree that's sometimes the case. There are simply times when you cross paths with someone who couldn't hold a conversation if their life depended on it. But, before you move on, ask yourself this: "Am I really asking the right questions?" Look at it this way — practically *everyone* is passionate about *something*. The problem is that you haven't asked the right questions to figure out what that is. I assure you when you figure it out, the conversation will become much easier and probably more interesting.

Before I share some illustrations on how you can make questions work for you, let me make one point absolutely clear. If you're asking questions just for the sake of "schmoozing" or to help disguise your personal agenda then it absolutely won't work. In fact, just the opposite will happen. You'll turn people away so fast you won't be able to keep track! Only when you have the mindset of pure curiosity — you're willing to ask questions and listen intently — can you learn more about the person you are talking to and appreciate them on a much deeper level. Good questions and careful listening will open your eyes and ears to people dropping verbal hints that others never seem to hear. These hints come in a variety of forms like "Let's meet next week after I get back from my trip" or "I can't make it to your meeting because we have to go to my kid's award ceremony." Do you see the hints? You may not care one lick about their travels or their kid's award ceremony. All you heard was a problem meeting your schedule. Here's the point: THEY care about it! So, stop and take the time to ask about the trip or the ceremony. They will appreciate you for it and work harder to give you more in return.

Growing up in the newspaper business, I was often tasked with selling ads to various businesses. When I look back at those times, I realize this was some of the best real world learning a young kid could have ever received. The last thing business owners want to see is another sales rep walk in their door. I had to quickly figure out how to not only get access to these owners but how to persuade them they needed to buy from me as well. Many times the same is true in conversations.

When I walked into a business owner's office, one of the first things I did was look around at the various pictures or trinkets on their desk or walls. This helped me discover what their passions were. Then I did what hardly anyone ever did — I asked them about it. There is no easier way to start a conversation (especially one involving spending money) than being truly interested in someone's specific passion. Because of this, I seldom had a difficult time establishing a connection with the client. Many times the person was more interested in buying from me versus other sales reps because of the questions I asked. Was my sales record 100%? Not even close, but I did a lot better than most others. What the other reps couldn't understand was that while they were calling on accounts, I was establishing relationships first; then I was selling advertising. On the occasions I didn't make the sale, I was usually in a position (owner's office) where at least I had the opportunity to present my product. They subconsciously knew that I was going to be working hard to sell them something, but they also knew that it would be enjoyable because I always took the time to let them talk about their favorite subjects — their passions and themselves.

I was in Montreal a while back talking to a friend who runs a private terminal at a major airport operation. His business is called an F.B.O. (Fixed Base Operation) where private aircraft owners park and hangar their planes when they arrive at the airport. His business is quite large and includes managing multi-million dollar jets. As my friend Zoran was touring me through his new facility, he pointed out a huge jet undergoing a complete refurbishment. The jet's unusual size created a conversation all by itself. Looking at it, he told me it was a new area he was taking his business into because of the significant profit margins in the retrofit side of the business. He said it had been mandatory that he take part in a bidding process in order to secure the two million dollar contract on the plane.

Here's where the story gets really interesting. He explained that he wasn't the lowest bidder but got the work anyway. Why? Because he did what no one else had done. Over the years, when the plane's owner had stopped into Zoran's FBO operation, he established a relationship with the owner of the plane and although he wasn't the cheapest, *he was the most trusted.* As Zoran said, "I got this work because of my relationship with the owner; in the end it had nothing to do with the bid." The same principles apply regardless of whether you're trying to secure a bid, land a new client or search for a job. Many times the winning company or person is the one who is the most known, liked and trusted. Being the cheapest isn't always the winning formula. As a matter of fact, it's often the losing one.

THINGS TO REMEMBER

THREE
Ask The Right Questions and Fill Your
Ocean of Knowledge

CHAPTER 10

What Goes Around Comes Around

Have you ever taken the time to look around and find that some people are getting a lot more lucky breaks than others? I'm not talking about the obvious ones, like celebrities or super rich people who always have a line of people waiting to help them. I'm talking about normal individuals who always seem to get a break when they need one. Let's examine this for a minute. I recently read a terrific book called *Never Eat Alone* that really brought home to me why luck has very little to do with getting breaks. It all boils down to this — you have to be willing to do things to help others without wanting anything in return. The "Great Circle Theory" — as I call it — begins by putting others' needs before your own. As I look back, I realize that many of the people who either help me or know someone who can when I am in a tight spot are ones I've helped with a problem years ago.

Here's a good example: I have been friends with a couple, Ed and Betsy Byars, for the last twenty years. Although Ed is accomplished in the world of mechanical engineering as well as an author of several books, he is simply a flying buddy to me. For the last twenty years, Ed and I have spent most of our time talking flying. What really sets Ed and Betsy apart is that their home sits in a community of homes that share a small landing strip. The nation is dotted with these kinds of places where people can live and fly from their own homes. About ten years ago, Ed received a call telling him that his little airport was too close to a bigger, major airport. Because of this perceived conflict, the state and county government decided they needed to shut down his airport. Ed and a few other owners had invested a lot of money and time into their cherished little community and quickly realized that this conflict would have to be resolved through the local and state politicians.

When I heard about the pending closure, I decided to put my connections and resources to work to help my friend. It took a couple of years, a lot of effort and a great deal of Ed's money for attorney's fees, but the order was finally removed. Ed's airport operates just fine to this day.

····························
Personal growth comes very fast if you begin to put others' needs first.
····························

Did I have to help Ed? Absolutely not. But it was the right thing to do and I did it expecting nothing in return. That's the critical part here — *doing things without expecting something in return.*

Years later, I was selling an airplane I had owned for five years and discovered that it had a previously unknown lien against it from a bank I had never heard of in Boston. Although the lien had long since been taken care of by a previous owner, it still marked the title, making the plane virtually unsellable. I was talking to Ed about the problem and, to my disbelief, he perked up and asked me which bank in Boston held the lien. I told him and he said, "No problem, one of my best friends is the president of that bank." We were about 800 miles away from Boston so needless to say, I was more than a little surprised. Ed proceeded to pick up the phone and explain the situation to his buddy. In a matter of minutes he fixed what would have taken me months to do. You just can't see that kind of thing coming!

Now I've decided to write a book, and I have access to something most aspiring authors only dream about — the ability to bounce ideas off Ed's wife, Betsy, who happens to be a best selling author of children's books. Some would consider this luck (and maybe it is), but I would relate it more to people's desire to help those who have helped them.

Another example of how a simple conversation can have results months later happened a while back when I had flown into Denver and was riding the dreaded shuttle bus to my hotel. There was just one other guy on the bus. I could have just sat there reading a book or diddling with my phone. Instead I asked him what brought him to Denver. He said he was the regional salesperson with Zimmer and was holding a conference for all of his sales reps. You've probably never heard of Zimmer. Me neither! Turns out, Zimmer sells medical equipment like titanium hips to orthopedic surgeons. A bus ride and a beer later, he had explained the entire system of selling medical equipment all the way down to what a sales rep makes per year. Now, if that were the end of the story, I would have at least walked away with a little more knowledge about the medical industry and a potential job idea if I was ever interested.

Fast-forward one year — my wife and I are at a friend's house in Birmingham, Alabama for a Christmas party. We live in South Carolina, so we didn't know anyone there except our friends and hosts, Dave and Jennifer. As usual, I'm going around talking to people, and it turns out several of them work for a medical supply company. I asked them if it was Zimmer, and with a shocked look, they told me they worked for Zimmer's competitor called Stryker. They couldn't believe I knew about Zimmer. It was obvious in their faces that they were thrilled to find someone who actually knew something about their work. As it turns out, we only talked about their job for a short time because they were much more interested in telling me about their real passion — inventing some very interesting new products.

The next hour was spent telling me about their ideas and giving me samples. An investment in their project might actually be in my future. This was all because I talked to a stranger on a bus in Denver.

On side note, I wrote that last paragraph while flying out west on a commercial flight chatting with a young man sitting next to me. He explained he was working on a masters in business at the University of Tennessee. I asked what else he did while attending college, and he told me he used to pole vault for the track team. Through more questions (I didn't know much about pole vaulting), I learned what it took to be a successful pole-vaulter. Besides a ton of courage, I discovered that injuries come with the sport as well. I finally asked him what his plans were after graduating. With my wide base of knowledge about various careers, I knew I had very high odds of knowing something about what he was going to say. Go figure, he said that because of his personal experience with broken bones and orthopedics, he wanted to sell medical devices for Stryker.

In the hopes of helping him, I threw him a bone and mentioned that I had just finished writing about some people I knew at Stryker and Zimmer in my new book. Like a blind dog, he walked right by the bone and said, "That's really interesting" and resumed watching his portable DVD player. I sat there smiling, knowing I could have provided him no less than three names of people currently in the industry, one of whom was a regional sales manager. All he had to do was have a minuscule amount of curiosity and ask me one or two questions. If he had, I wonder where his career would be today. Did it bother me that he didn't want any help in his job search? Not really. But, when he graduates and starts sending resumes to companies he will probably be walking down the long road to business success, which is discussed in Part III.

You must understand that personal growth comes very fast if you begin to put others' needs first and start developing more curiosity toward them. I just showed you how helping someone out rescued me several years later, and how a casual meeting on a hotel bus had an impact on numerous people and two different potential deals. *Now multiply that by fifty or more a year!* It quickly becomes apparent how networks can add up and how breaks can start coming your way if you start expanding your horizons. Remember, if you're not genuinely curious about other people's lives, you really won't have a chance at getting them to open up and take a liking to you. The reverse tends to happen if you go on and on about yourself. You will become a bore to them causing them to eliminate you from the conversation. Think about it — people who are selfish and lacking in curiosity are usually the ones who always say they're "unlucky" or just can't get a break in their life. Why? Because all they think and talk about is themselves.

If you want to watch a movie that really highlights how putting others first and getting involved can have the "Great Circle" effect on your life, I would recommend the movie "Yes Man" starring Jim Carey. Usually there isn't much to gain from his movies other than some laughs, but this particular movie struck a chord with me because of its incredible hidden meaning. The point of the story is that his life stunk in every area because he said "No" to just about every person and opportunity he stumbled across. One day he decided to say "Yes" to everything that came his way. More importantly, he started to put others' needs before his own. Remarkably, his life began to change for the better almost immediately, and breaks he never thought possible opened up for him. He saw that by helping people out, by saying "Yes" when they are in need, they come back to help him with critical things in his life. Think about this for a moment: what are you saying "No" to in your life right now? Are there people out there you could help or places you've avoided going because it's just not comfortable for you?

Does simply saying "Yes" sound too good to be true? Let me give you an example of how saying "Yes" and helping people has led me down paths I couldn't have imagined in my wildest dreams. About fifteen years ago, there was a guy named Lindsey Graham working as a small town attorney where I ran a newspaper. Other than talking socially through various clubs, we really didn't know each other that well. One day, Lindsey came to my office to discuss his desire to run for political office and be state representative for our district. After several hours of talking, I began to understand how passionate he was to be successful in politics. He asked me to help him personally as well as have the newspaper I co-owned with my family back him in his bid for the seat. I was convinced he was the kind of guy we needed at the statehouse, so I worked hard using the newspaper and my time to help him win the seat.

End of story, right? Wrong! Lindsey stayed in the statehouse for a few years before he saw an opportunity to run for the U.S. House of Representatives in Washington, D.C. He was elected to the seat and spent the next four years establishing himself as an up-and-coming politician. Through a unique set of circumstances, he had an opportunity to run for the U.S. Senate in 2002. Again, he won easily and has since become not only one of the most powerful people in U.S. politics, but he has made a name for himself across the nation and the world!

During this time we remained good friends and even vacationed together on occasion. I never once thought what committee he could put me on or how I could use his success to bolster my own. I simply did what I believed to be the right thing to do. Along our travels, he introduced me to another Washington friend of his named Mark Sanford. We all became friends and before I knew it, Mark was the Governor of my state!

Understanding how you can meet a person's needs is a key networking point.

The Governor of any state obviously has a lot of friends. The question no one ever asks is "How did you get to be such good friends with our state's Governor that you hang out and vacation together frequently?" One day early in our friendship, Mark and I were talking and he told me he enjoyed being Governor, but he truly disliked being invited to events where everyone wanted *him* to come but not his wife and kids. He said it was tough coming home virtually every night not being able to see his kids before they went to bed. Being a father myself, his comments struck a nerve with me. I would hate to constantly be missing out on important things I do with my wife and kids. Because of this, I made sure that whenever I invited him for a football game or anything else, I always invited the rest of his family. Did he appreciate it? Absolutely! In return, he invited my family down to the Governor's mansion for sleepovers and other amazing adventures. Because of this initial realization of his needs, he and I spent a lot of time together and are now good friends who do things with and without our families. Here's the point — most people never figured that out. Instead, they all just think I'm lucky to be such good friends with someone like him.

I've learned over the last year that being friends with the Governor can come back to bite you when he makes national news by committing adultery. When he called me to apologize for being such a lousy friend and a poor example as the leader of our state, I told him that I was never his friend because he was the Governor, and this would give me a chance to prove it. However, I went on to tell him he was about to find out who his true friends really were! People forget that it's easy being friends when things are going great, but the real test of friendship is when the train goes off the tracks. I believe a true friend sticks with you through good times *and bad* – something many people don't understand. We all make lousy decisions from time to time, some are just more visible than others. Regardless, to this day Mark and I talk regularly and take trips together. I still count him as my friend and I know he would say the same.

In the world of networking, it might be impressive to say you're friends with people like Lindsey Graham and Mark Sanford, but the real power comes in who *they* are friends with. When I get invited to their private functions the incredible people I am able to connect with is nothing short of amazing. Again, the point is it all started by simply saying "Yes" to helping a friend. Did I have to help him? No! Did I expect anything from it? No! That was over fifteen years ago. A few months ago Lindsey and I attended a grand opening, and he made it obvious that he hadn't forgotten my help years ago when he spent over fifteen minutes of his speech recounting how I helped him begin his quest to be what he is today.

Whether you network with your neighbor or a U.S. Senator, curiosity and generosity can and will always be rewarded. It may take a day; it may take 20 years, but I believe that what goes around, comes around — that's the principle of the "Great Circle".

I tell these stories in an attempt to bring home the fact that people and adventures like this one do not just magically come your way. People often ask how I'm so lucky to be able to do so many interesting and unique things in my life. The fact remains that luck has very little to do with it. You simply need to be someone who is interested in others more than you are yourself. If you couple that with a willingness to say "Yes" more than "No," you will be surprised how things change in your life. So the next time you see someone doing something you'd love to do, take a minute to ask them to break down *exactly* how they got themselves in that position. That's where the real learning is!

THINGS TO REMEMBER

FOUR
Say Yes

FIVE
Put Others First and Start Building
Your Own "Great Circle"

CHAPTER 11

I've Got This One

One of the unfortunate by-products of enjoying success in life is starting to believe you're simply too smart to fail. I would love to say that I've never succumbed to this state of mind, but I would be lying. When your years of work are met with financial rewards, it's easy to believe you're one of the smartest people on the planet. I guess that, much like in sports, if you don't fall down once in a while you're not trying hard enough. The problem is that in sports, you dust yourself off, nurse your injuries and learn from the mistake. In business, you're not dirty or hurt — at least not physically. No, the mistakes made in business tend to hurt your bank account and ego more than anything. Let me reluctantly tell you a few of my mistakes in the hopes that some lessons can be gleaned.

I always thought that nothing could be more unique than being able to call yourself an inventor. After all, how many people really can say they invented something that is part of everyone's daily life. Being a tall guy, I was tired of having to twist and turn in the shower to stay wet and warm. One day I went to the hardware store and bought some PVC pipe and created what I thought was the most brilliant thing mankind had ever seen — the ability to turn a single shower head into a double-headed one, hence eliminating all the twisting and turning. Over the years, I created some crude examples of what a double-headed showerhead could look like in its final form. Knowing it would take money I didn't have, I put it on the back burner and continued showering with my PVC contraption. That's where I should have stopped. In the late 90's, our company sold some of our media properties in the Midwest which gave us the financial ability to diversify the company. Although my main focus was taking our company into the field of commercial development, I couldn't help thinking that I could now afford to bring my beautiful creation to fruition.

I spent many long hours doing all the things you would expect in bringing my "Twinjet" dual showerhead to market; I just had no idea how expensive it would be. I had a computerized design done, very expensive molds created for the injection plastic manufacturer, packaging designed — you name it I did it. Over a hundred thousand dollars later, I had a product that I believed was wonderful and performed exactly how I expected it would. It was then I realized that I had made a mistake. Can you guess what it was? Here's a hint — remember the old saying, there's no "I" in "team." I was so confident that I knew exactly what everyone desired in a shower system that I didn't even bother (heck, it never even crossed my mind) to gather up about ten very sharp people in my network and buy them dinner while I picked their brains on what they thought was the perfect system. Nope, just "me, myself and I" were going to do this one.

You can probably already see how this story ends. Even though my product was featured in about every major newspaper and bath magazine in the country, it still sold poorly. Even though the idea of two showerheads was liked by many (just go to any Westin Hotel and see for yourself), my design and use of plastic as the main material was a major turnoff to most people. Would the result have been different had I brought my network together to get some outside opinions? I would like to think so. All I have to show for it is a three ring binder full of news clippings, a lot less money in the bank and a whole bunch of extra showerheads left to sell. The bottom line is this — I screwed up because I thought I was smarter than I was, and I forgot to use my network to verify my thinking.

·····························
A network is useless if you don't use it ... period.
·····························

It seems to take me about ten years to start thinking I'm smarter than I am. By 2006 more success than failure had come my way. I felt it was time to start reaching out into some new areas. Many of my friends were making a ton of money developing residential neighborhoods, so when a friend approached me with a plan to do one of our own I couldn't help but take a hard look at it. I had done some commercial and office development in the past and found it to be rather straightforward. However, I had never done a residential subdivision. For some help and advice, my friend assembled a team of three other guys who seemed to have experience with residential development.

The problem was only two of the guys had developed subdivisions before, and none of them were very successful. In short, we found a great site and a year later built a wonderful subdivision — right as the real estate market tanked. Although market timing was a significant cause for the failure, I really don't believe it was the main one. The reality of the situation is the subdivision never should have been built. I should have taken the time to talk to no less than a dozen of my friends who are literally experts in the world of residential development as well as the economy. From them, I would have discovered that not only was a real estate crash coming, but my subdivision wouldn't have made it in good times or bad. Any one of these people could have run some simple numbers for me and shown me why I wasn't going to sell nearly enough home sites to be successful. Although the numbers were simple to them, they were foreign to me.

The bottom line is that a network is useless if you don't use it...period. One of the main checkpoints I now have before starting a new project is going through my complete list of friends in order to identify who has expertise in that given area. I buy them dinner and pick their heads clean of all they know. The most expensive dinner is still far cheaper than losing a bunch of money on a deal out of ego and ignorance.

Let me finish this chapter by showing you what certain people in your network can do to aid a deal when you simply ask them for help. The prime corner of commercial real estate in my hometown had sat empty for years with a giant mound of dirt covering a majority of the land. Although I had driven by it every day for the last ten years and had seen the little "For Sale" sign sitting on it, it never occurred to me to call the number and actually try to buy such a large piece of land.

One day my father mentioned it wouldn't hurt to look at what the situation was with the property. I figured the worst thing that could happen was to hear "No," so I made a phone call to the realtor and found out who owned it. Being somewhat naive to these situations, I did what I simply felt most comfortable doing; I went to the owner's house and rang his doorbell. I introduced myself and explained what I was there for. He was a lonely retired doctor in his eighties who saw me as welcome company, so he invited me in for a cup of coffee to discuss the subject further. Over the next two months, we had five of the longest three hour meetings in my life. We spent 90% of the meeting talking about his career as a doctor and his many accomplishments and the last 10% discussing my desire to buy his land.

This time I was smarter. A good friend of mine was a developer who had put together many large commercial land purchases. I went to see Bill and asked him how I should structure a major land purchase like this. Surprisingly, he knew the doctor and told me he was definitely interested in selling this property, as well as another property nearby. With Bill's guidance, I had all the information I needed to create a deal that was a win-win for everyone.

At the last meeting with the doctor, I came prepared with a purchase contract. Not only did he sign it for both pieces of land, he even went so far as to hug me and wish me well. He got the price he wanted, and I got the opportunity to develop the property and increase its value ten times beyond the original price.

The biggest surprise of all came when I learned that every major developer in a five county area had already tried to buy the land from him but couldn't get the deal done. In my opinion they were missing two things — the willingness to spend hours listening to someone else's story (remember everyone's favorite subject) and, most importantly, they didn't have a friend like Bill to help them know where all the hot buttons were.

THINGS TO REMEMBER

SIX
Connect With Your Network to
Expand Your Knowledge Base

SEVEN
Splurge for Dinner to Save Costly Mistakes

EIGHT
It's Not About You!

IN A NUTSHELL
8 Ways To Grow An Amazing Network Of Friends

ONE
It's What You Know About Who You Know

TWO
Everyone Wants To Talk About Their
Passions — Let Them

THREE
Ask The Right Questions and Fill Your
Ocean Of Knowledge

FOUR
Say Yes

FIVE
Put Others First and Start Building
Your Own "Great Circle"

SIX
Connect With Your Network to Expand
Your Knowledge Base

SEVEN
Splurge For Dinner to
Save Costly Mistakes

EIGHT
It's Not About You!

PART III
It Depends on
YOU!

" If it was easy, everyone would do it. "

{Another Steve-ism}

Part III • It Depends on You!

CHAPTER 12

Choices...Choices...Choices

I t's the choices you make and the chances you take that determine your destiny!

Have you ever thought about life that way? When you really break it down, everything in life — both good and bad — comes down to your choices. One of the greatest motivational speakers of all time, Jim Rohn, said, "Everything in life is easy to do...it's also just as easy NOT to do it."

Think about that. Every day we make hundreds if not thousands of choices. We wake up and choose what to wear, who to call, what to eat, where we need to be, when to be somewhere and the list goes on and on. What we tend to forget is that although many of those decisions are mundane, many are not. One thing is for sure...our choices literally determine our destiny.

I have often compared the choices we make in life to an organizational chart you see in many companies. The chart always starts with the top ranking person and spreads downward like branches of a tree to show where all the rest of the staff rank in their respective positions. Much like a corporation, our life choices run on similar paths except you need to imagine two corporations (trees) standing side by side with a few branches connecting the two of them. One corporation is operating with great growth, success and wealth while the other is running with negative growth, poor results and is losing money. We all exist within these "trees of life" and our decisions will determine whether or not your life bears the amazing fruit of success or the bitter taste of average.

If you engage (See Part II) any successful person and drill down on their history, I guarantee they will tell you that they made a series of good decisions at critical points in their life, which ultimately determined what they are today. Stop for a minute and think of someone — anyone — you admire or yearn to be more like. If you put your jealousy away and look at them from an objective standpoint you will discover that they were either consciously or subconsciously making solid decisions throughout their entire life. I'm also willing to bet they have a tremendous circle of quality friends and family around them that helped them stay aligned with strong values and beliefs along the way.

....
The past does not equal the future.
....

We all make bad decisions in life, but the trick is to recognize the choice as a poor one and make immediate corrections so you can jump back over to the good side of the hierarchy. Even though we all make bad decisions from time to time, it's critical to remember that a few bad decisions do not mean you're doomed for failure the rest of your life. I always say, "The past does not equal the future." Unfortunately, many people make poor decisions that can't be undone without major repercussions in their life. Poor, irrevocable decisions are saying "I do" to the wrong person or being young, single and accidentally getting pregnant. Things like that aren't easily remedied by simply changing course. I see it happen within people's careers as well.

I live in a town with a major college university and a football program that is often ranked nationally. Last year there was a defensive lineman who had everything going for him in the world of football. At 6'8" and over 300 pounds he was an enormous specimen of a guy who had worked his whole life to make succeeding in football his number one priority. It was working, too. He was often described as the core of the line with unlimited potential to make it in the NFL. He was rapidly climbing the success hierarchy and things were looking great for him until one fateful night when a poor decision took it all away. He was in a bar and one of the patrons decided to badger him on a personal level (which took either a ton of courage or a ton of stupidity) and got him mad enough that a fight erupted. Common sense says that when you pick a fight with a mountain of a man, things usually don't go well for the opposing party. This was no exception. The football player beat the guy within an inch of his life and was hauled off and charged by the police. What was the result of that one poor choice? He was permanently kicked off the football team and even worse, this violation eliminated him from transferring to play for other colleges. Basically, the thousands of hours of blood, sweat and tears he put into his football career ended that night in the bar.

If the above example isn't clear enough for you, take another look at the first sentence of this chapter. It was given to me by one of his teammates who is experiencing success at every level in his life. "The choices you make and the chances you take WILL determine your destiny." I guarantee it! Don't ever think your choices don't matter!

Take a minute and think of someone you know who is successful in life. I don't care if they are wealthy business people, great athletes or the best parents in the world. I guarantee you their success didn't just happen. Instead, they chose to work every single day on becoming better at whatever they wanted to succeed in. None of them will tell you that they instantly became as good as they are now. More importantly, none of them expected instant success. Most will say that over time they mastered the skills required, and amazing things have come their way from it. I'm sorry to be the one to tell you, but there isn't an easy button. Success in anything requires you to take it one step at a time. The good news is that it's not as many steps away as you might think...

you just have to keep stepping! Let me say that again...you just have to keep stepping! The difference is most people aren't willing to do it. Instead, they want success to come easy and to happen right now! Just go into a gas station and watch endless people come in and spend money buying a ticket to the lottery. Successful people often say the lottery is the retirement plan for the poor. So why then if all that is required is to keep stepping toward your goal most people don't find success? Good question! The answer can be found back in Jim Rohn's quote at the beginning of this chapter. "It's just as easy NOT to do it."

Which leads us into the area of desire...

THINGS TO REMEMBER

ONE
Choices Determine Your Destiny

CHAPTER 13

You've Gotta Want It

Why do some people make great choices while others make choices that lead to miserable failures? I believe with all my heart, that it all comes down to one word — DESIRE. At the end of the day you can have all the curiosity about others and the personal responsibility in the world, but if you don't want it then it doesn't really matter.

I often ask audiences to imagine they are in a room made of nothing but concrete. Floors, ceiling, walls, everything is solid concrete. I ask them how they would react if I told them they had fifteen minutes to get out of the room. The audience usually has the "deer in the headlights" look because they know that it would be virtually impossible to escape such conditions. Sure, they would tap and maybe kick on the walls a little, but in the end they would be stuck in the room. Then I radically change the scenario...

Once they have all become comfortable with the fact that they would be in this fantasy concrete room until help arrived I say, "Now imagine that your oxygen runs out in fifteen minutes... you're dead in fifteen minutes." The audience's eyes light up and their expression grows fierce almost immediately. They know it's a game changer and all bets are off. They agree with me that they would now be doing things that would be considered crazy in normal circumstances. They would be banging and scraping the walls with every piece of furniture in the room and even clawing at it with their fingernails.

The point is that when you want something that bad...that's where amazing is! Do you see it? When you really want something that bad, it doesn't matter if you've been formally trained in it or have a degree in it. All that matters is that you are willing to do whatever it takes to accomplish your goal. Unfortunately, most people don't understand this and sometimes even expect it to just be handed to them. I've got bad news. Life doesn't work that way for any of us.

Stop and think for a minute about something amazing that happened in your life. I don't care how big or little it is. I guarantee you this, it didn't just magically happen. Almost everything amazing that happens in people's lives is because somewhere, in the process, they decided they wanted it. From there, their choices and desire combined to make an unbeatable combination for success.

Early in my speaking career I was talking to audiences that ranged in size from thirty to ninety people. I decided to take a couple of days off in order to go to a large retreat my church was putting on in Daytona Beach, Florida. This was a huge youth retreat for over fifteen hundred kids. Because I was friends with the church's senior staff, I was allowed to tour the stage one night prior to the big concert and sermon. One of my friends ushered me onto the stage and let me look out into the sea of empty chairs that would be filled in a matter of hours. As I stood there I knew one thing for sure...and I knew it with absolute certainty. I knew that someday in my future I would be the one on a stage sharing my positive message with thousands of people. As I stood there silently looking out over the chairs I could vividly see myself doing it. My friend had no idea what I was doing and was getting tired of waiting so he said, "Hey, let's head on out of here." I simply held up my hand and told him I needed a few more minutes to stand there. When he asked why, I told him with pure conviction in my voice, that somewhere in my future (I was assuming five years) I would be impacting that many people with my beliefs.

End of story? Not hardly! From there I kept stepping...and stepping. I kept making decisions to do whatever I had to do in order to continue on the road to becoming a speaker and author of national importance. When you make a decision to do whatever it takes and implement the right choices to make it happen you actually start wielding the power to blow right through the concrete walls.

Surprisingly, a mere three months later I received a phone call asking me to be the opening speaker at an event that would be in an arena with three thousand people. I had to face three major problems right away, 1) I had no speech prepared for that particular audience 2) There were going to be twenty nine hundred more people than I had ever spoken to and 3) I had three days to prepare. Wow! Many people would have just done the easy thing and said, "No" to the invitation. I didn't. I had no idea how I was going to pull it off, but I knew I had more than enough desire to make it happen. I had just met a speaking coach (that day) and asked her to take a chance on me and help me through the process. In the end I worked night and day (literally) to make it happen. I had a coach and a ton of friends that poured everything into my effort of achieving the success I desired.

··························

I will do anything I have to do in order for this to be a success!

··························

Two days before my twenty minute speech, I was in a late afternoon meeting with my new coach, and I'll never forget the trepidation she had on her face when she told me that in order for me to accomplish her "to do" list, I was going to have to be up most of the night. I really think she was startled at my response which was basically, "I will do *anything* I have to do in order for this to be a success!" She got the point very clearly.

In the end, I spent well over forty hours in three days preparing for a twenty minute speech. I gave it in front of three thousand people and got a standing ovation! As I stood there soaking in the loud applause, one thing struck me. All the work and stress that it took to make this happen in the previous days was a distant memory compared to the amazing happening right in front of me!

Would it have been just as easy to say, "No" and keep on coasting through life? Absolutely! But that's not where true amazing is! Amazing in any aspect of your life requires "Yes, and then following through with absolute desire.

What is it in your life that you want so bad you would blow through concrete walls to get it? Take a minute and think about it. When you find it, whether it's a person, place or thing, nothing in the world can stop you from achieving it!

Desire wins every time!

THINGS TO REMEMBER

TWO
Desire Wins Every Time

CHAPTER 14

Just Be Different

Whenever I watch a game show on TV, I always wonder how the contestants end up getting picked over the thousands of others wishing for the same opportunity. I discovered the answer one day when I made friends with a lady who was actually chosen to be a contestant on a major game show. Instead of being jealous of her opportunity or just writing her off as lucky, I did the unthinkable — I asked her to sit down and tell me exactly how she managed to pull off such a feat. She told me that while they stood in line outside the studio, the producers had several people walking around engaging people. My new friend quickly figured out that the people who stood out in one form or fashion were going to catch someone's eye and gain a much better chance of being chosen. So, that's exactly what she did. She began singing and dancing like her life depended on it. Most people didn't have the courage or the talent to do something so outlandish, but she was determined to be a contestant. Because of it, she got picked and went on to do something most of us only dream of. I guess she just wanted it more. Makes you think, doesn't it?

How about this, a friend of mine who works at a major industrial plant told me a story about a guy who interviewed with his company. This interviewee came in and went through the normal interview process of answering all the appropriate questions and asking some of his own. Nothing was out of the ordinary until the end. That's when the applicant took out one of his business cards and lit it on fire. He let it get a good flame going (as I'm sure the interviewer sat there in disbelief), and then he took a big breath and blew the fire out. He looked up at the shocked interviewer and said with complete conviction, "Hire me and I'll be your dragon slayer...nothing will stop me from success." Without a doubt, the guy had a lot of charisma to pull off such a stunt, and he succeeded in his objective. He differentiated himself from every other candidate vying for the job. He was revered for being able to pull off a stunt like that with such confidence. Guess what? The company offered him the job! I'm not saying you need to go light random fires and then impress people with your extinguishing skills (really...don't do this) but I am saying you need to do something to differentiate yourself from everyone else.

When I speak to audiences full of salespeople, I often ask them a simple question. "Why should I pick you?" My point is that the buying public is always having to decide which salesperson to buy from, which store to go to or which brand to buy. Why should they pick yours? Typically, people revert to the easy answer of, "They like me more" or "Everyone knows we offer the best merchandise". My personal favorite is "I'll work harder for you than anyone else". They all seem shocked when I tell them every single person in the room will tell me the exact same answer! So, I ask again, "Why should I pick you?"

Being able to differentiate yourself isn't as hard as most people think, and it hardly ever requires a song and dance routine! The bar is so low in our society that standing out really isn't that hard. Just being someone who is willing to take personal responsibility for their own actions while being truly curious about others and engaging people on a much more personal level puts you light years ahead of most. But, when you add pure desire to the mix it's like the spark to gunpowder. A huge explosion of amazing happens.

I had a friend call me a week ago with some extremely kind words for the message I convey in both my writing as well as my presentations. He swore that I was the reason his life went from average to amazing over the last year. After he went on for quite a while (I wasn't in a rush to stop him), I had to make a confession to him. I told him I didn't bring any amazing into his life. I simply showed him the door, and he made the conscious decision to walk through it. Remember — it's easy to do it and it's just as easy not to. The point is that when you look at your life objectively and decide it isn't where you want it to be, you become extremely motivated to change it. His motivation has led to a dramatic increase in his sales career as well as improvement in his personal life. He just did it.

···

If you want to differentiate yourself from any crowd all you have to do is quit being plain vanilla.

···

Remember, if you want to differentiate yourself from any crowd all you have to do is quit being plain vanilla. Do you think Ben and Jerry's ice cream makers would be famous today if they came out with their three big, fancy, fantastic flavors of chocolate, vanilla and strawberry? No way. So what did they do? They came out with flavors no one had ever heard of before — brownie batter, chubby hubby, chunky monkey and the list goes on! Is their ice cream any better than any other major manufacturers? I'm not an ice cream expert but I doubt it. It's just different!

Go out and create some Ben and Jerry's in your life!

THINGS TO REMEMBER

THREE
People Choose You When You Stand Out

CHAPTER 15

Show Me The Money

When I was in high school, a family friend who was a banker asked me a seemingly simple question: "How much money would it take for you to be rich?" Think about that for a minute — what's your answer? I sat there for several minutes trying to spout out a dollar amount that would make sense, but my mind was like a computer caught in an endless loop, unable to solve the problem. My confusion turned to embarrassment (I'm sure it was amusing watching me work at warp speed trying to solve the question) because I was never able to give him an answer. The reality is I'm not sure there really is an answer. I believe it's a moving target that constantly changes, causing us to struggle with it our entire life. I also believe that's a good thing. Let me explain.

We've all heard the old adage that, "Money doesn't create happiness." I totally agree with that cliché, but no one ever tells you the rest of the story. Money *does* create freedom. Although happiness can come from many different areas in your life, you will never have the freedom to do all the things that can provide wonderful experiences for you and the people around you without some financial strength. I recently read a survey that asked two hundred married couples what was the number one thing causing stress in their marriage. Overwhelmingly it was the lack of money!

Let's start with some of the basics to success and wealth. I read a book a while back called The Millionaire Mind by Thomas Stanley. In the book there was one statistic that stood out. He asked 700 millionaires what they believed the number one trait was that helped them achieve their success. Any guesses what the number one trait was? Was it working long hours or earning a Master's Degree from a prestigious college? Nope. It was excellent, interpersonal communication skills. The simple ability to communicate effectively comes in first, every time. If you think about it, you really shouldn't be surprised. There are many aspects to being successful but nothing is more important than a solid ability to communicate and connect with people. Guess what? Most people can't do it. Why? Because they are poor listeners and don't know the right questions to ask to make a conversation flow. I talked about this in the chapter about everyone's favorite subject. It might be worth your time to read it again. I'm not saying if your communication skills are lousy you'll never experience success and wealth, but I guarantee you that your particular road to success will be much longer than it is for those who can communicate effectively.

Money does create freedom.

Ultimately, we all know being rich does not require being financially wealthy. While that is a true statement, my focus in this section is to help you not only be more successful in your work, but to see financial gains from it as well. Doing so requires an understanding of some basic principles covered in the following chapters. One thing is for sure — one of the main reasons people step into the business world is to make more money than they could have otherwise. What's missing in our education system — as well as most parenting — is some "real" lessons on how to speed up the rate at which your financial success happens. The result can be a life that doesn't involve the constant fear of bills and debts. Let me say that again. Although most of us have bills and debts of some nature, you have to realize that the stress comes into play when you don't have the money to pay them. Most people go about fixing this by getting a job. That's a good start, but the real key to freedom is creating your own success.

THINGS TO REMEMBER

FOUR
Great Communication Creates Great Wealth
In All Areas Of Your Life

CHAPTER 16

Making Connections

Many people who are struggling in their lives tend to justify their problems with the mindset that successful people are simply the lucky ones who just catch all the breaks. If you're struggling in life I would challenge you to stop and think for a minute about the times in your life when you did have success professionally or the times you've experienced great things on a personal level. If you stop and analyze it, I'm willing to bet you will realize that only about 30% of the professional success and amazing adventures happened due to your hard work. What people typically don't realize is that the other 70% has happened by others giving it to you. Let me explain. Without the ability to make strong, lasting connections it becomes extremely difficult to create much success in any aspect of your life. If you approach everything with an "army of one" mindset I assure you that you will get just that, a lonely life with only yourself to talk to. Why? Because whether you're job hunting, selling a product or building your own business, without others helping you and offering up their circle of influence it will be very hard, if not impossible, to create the success you wish for.

If you sat down with any successful person I guarantee you would find that they are using certain strategies to create positive outcomes in their lives as well as the people they network with. When it comes to expanding your network one strategy people often overlook is to simply notice things that others either don't care about or just don't see. This can be as simple as looking at a person's name badge in a store and then do the unthinkable –

care enough to start calling them by name. Many times the person forgets they are even wearing a name badge and gives you much better customer service because they either feel more connected to you or are trying to figure out how you know them! Either way they appreciate being called by name versus saying, "Hey you! I need some help over here." I didn't fully realize this until a friend of mine was watching me in a hardware store keying off of employees name tags and then talking to them on a first name basis. After we got the information I needed, my friend commented that it was incredible how the service level went up exponentially when I addressed the person by name.

Another way to make connections with strangers is to look at how they dress for clues. A few months ago I was attending a presentation about an investment opportunity for a new, state-of-the-art fire extinguisher. The company was looking for investors who could help propel them to capture a larger share of the fire extinguisher market. About twenty minutes before their presentation was to begin, I was walking down a hallway and came across a guy named Josh who was wearing some clothing that caught my eye. His baseball cap had Ping, a famous golf club maker's name on it. The name was also mongrammed on three different parts of his shirt. Remember, I was at a fire demonstration and golf had nothing to do with it. Yet, here is this guy who had the golf club maker's name plastered all over himself. Without hesitation, I simply asked him with a slight tone of sarcasm in my voice, "Are you sponsored by Ping or what?" He smiled and looked at me and said, "Why, yes I am." Now it was my turn to be surprised so I went on to ask him exactly what he did for Ping. He showed me some incredible videos of his golf show that incorporates a motivational message. He's one of the few people in the world who could hit out of this world golf trick shots and incorporates a motivational message to go with his show. After about ten minutes of talking we agreed to meet for lunch a few days later. Over lunch and several more meetings we not only grew as friends, but our families did as well. To this day, he is a great friend who helps me in my speaking career as well as my golf game. On top of that, it turns out that he's friends with the producer from the hit TV show "The Amazing Race" and thinks there could be a real possibility that he and I could participate on the show. How amazing is that? That's a great example of the 70% that others offer up to you. You just can't see that kind of thing coming! Here's the learning point. I could have kept my mouth shut and walked right by him. If I had, an amazing individual with a whole host of things available to help me advance my career would have walked right by! That's where I see so many people lose out on amazing opportunities. They don't engage people and in return what could have been an incredible moment turns into nothing at all.

·····························

Connecting with people on a significant level requires one-on-one, face-to-face communication.

·····························

A final way to create better connections with people is to just get in front of them. What I mean is that our society has become one that defaults toward hiding behind a computer or phone screen. Almost everyone seems happy to text, e-mail, Facebook or tweet, but when it comes to face-to-face conversations, many people seem to be shying away (pun intended). Just look at teenagers today. Do you ever hear their phone actually ring? No! But, they can type away on their phone at lightning speed! The concerning result I see of this is a diminishing of interpersonal communication skills. Although I find electronic communication to be highly effective at times, I don't rely on it. I still believe if you truly want to connect with people on a significant level, it requires one-on-one, face-to-face communication. I know people have hundreds, if not thousands of friends on Facebook, or at least they think they do. I don't know how you define a friend but I doubt too many of your friends on Facebook would really come to your rescue and bail you out of a tough situation. Don't believe me? Just send out a request for a short term loan! They won't give it to you, but will be more than happy to let everyone on Facebook know you're having a tough time! Here's the bottom line. In order to establish lasting connections that enable you to release the 70% of the amazing left untapped, you have to be willing to engage people with noticing strategies and techniques that only work in a real, face-to-face environment.

Another mistake people make in establishing enduring relationships is that they start taking them for granted. There's not much worse than having a friend who hasn't bothered to talk to you in a long time, call you and ask a favor. If you want people to stay connected with you then you have to do things that keep the bond strong. I always drop people a personalized, handwritten thank you note to let them know I appreciate their efforts to help me. I am constantly carving out time in my schedule in order take both new and existing friends out for breakfast or lunch. Remarkably, when I need a favor, the connection is strong enough for me to not only feel comfortable asking for it, but knowing they will absolutely respond.

One last method (and the most effective) of keeping relationships strong is a point I lightly referenced back in Chapter 10. Take the time and make the effort to look at things from the other person's perspective. We live in such a me, me, me world, that if you just start putting the needs of others first, and start thinking from a you, you, you mindset, a lot of positive change will come your way...but it doesn't happen immediately. Wait! I want it NOW you say...well sorry to be the bearer of bad news but it just doesn't happen that way. The good news is that when the circle is complete and someone gives back to you, it becomes wonderfully obvious that it was worth being patient.

Giving without expecting anything in return starts a process I have affectionately named "The Great Circle" and like anything worthwhile, it takes time for the circle to complete itself and develop into something special. However, a point many miss is that the only way this technique works is to start the process. While most people are wallowing around feeling sorry for themselves and wondering why they never seem to catch a break, others are living an amazing life and seem to have people wanting to help them at every corner! I assure you they started the great circle in their past and are experiencing the rewards of people doing incredible things for them now. So, how do you start it? Try this. Find an opportunity to help someone out with something that most people would say "No" to. I don't care if it's helping them move a piano or find a new job. Help them with all your time and resources. Remember it's easy to say "No" but it requires a degree of getting uncomfortable to say "Yes."

Here's a couple of examples. A few years back I was kicking back reading the USA Today newspaper and came across an article about an organization in my own state that was working tirelessly saving animals all over the country from certain death. The organization was called Pilots N Paws and was designed to solicit the help of airplane owners who would be willing to use their airplanes (for free) to fly to "kill shelters" which is an animal shelter where they keep the dogs and cats for a very short period of time and then euthanize them. The mission of this organization is to fly in, extract the animals who were unknowingly on death row, and fly them to cities where they keep them until they can find them new homes and a much brighter future.

Because my airplane often has available cargo room, I didn't hesitate to pick up the phone and offer my plane up for any missions they might have. I was surprised when the director thanked me profusely for calling her since she had no pilots in my area of the state ever offer up help of any kind (remember about people usually not willing to start the great circle). As promised, a few weeks later she called to ask if I would fly a trip from a neighboring town with three dogs to some families wishing to adopt them three states away. Again, it would have been very easy just to say "No" but I did what I promised and agreed to spend my time and money doing a good deed. This could (and probably should) be the end of the story — one person doing a good deed for another. But the great circle often times works in mysterious ways! A few days after agreeing to fly the trip she called me back and said that she had just received a call from Good Morning America and they wanted to do a story on this particular flight. She went on to ask me if I would mind being featured live on their morning broadcast! It only took a split second for me to say absolutely! From there things snowballed, and I was able to have not only myself but my daughter and niece with me during the broadcast. We all felt pretty special not only saving the lives of three dogs but receiving an experience very few people ever enjoy. All because I decided to do something without wanting anything in return!

Here's another example that might bring this point home to you. One evening just before sunset, I took my son out for a ride in the country in an old sports car. We stopped for a minute to appreciate the beauty of the sunset, and that's when things went downhill. I turned off the car not realizing the battery wasn't strong enough to start it again. With nightfall coming fast I did what any self respecting father would do — I told my son to get out and push the car while I showed him how to pop the clutch and jumpstart the car! He did a great job and pushed us down the little hill we were perched on. I popped the clutch and the car didn't even think about starting. As we rolled to a stop at the bottom of the hill I knew we were probably in for a long night unless we could convince someone to help us out. Several cars went by us and never even tapped their brakes. Then a young man with his wife and kids in tow pulled over and offered some help. I explained my situation, and he gladly jumped the battery with his jumper cables. I was so thrilled I handed him my business card (I don't know why) and thanked him profusely.

End of story? Nope. The circle was only half complete.

Three weeks later my brother and I were cutting the ribbon on our new press facility and there was a large crowd of dignitaries there for the occasion. As I was milling around talking to people I was shocked to come across the young man who had come to my rescue weeks earlier. Needless to say, I was glad to see him! He explained that he was working to get some business from our company and wanted to come by to see our new facility. Until then, he had never made the connection between me and the company whose business he so badly wanted to earn. I gave him my card (again) and personally introduced him to the managers in my company that he needed to meet. I then gave them instructions to help him get what he needed in ANY way possible! Circle complete. Of course, he could have just driven by me like everyone else. Then he would have been just another face in the crowd wondering why he couldn't get a break!

Start creating new circles in your life today! It might take a few days or a few years for the circle to complete itself, but when it does you'll be astonished at the wonderful outcome! Even if the person you help isn't ever in a position to help you out they could very well know someone who is. Remember...everyone is connected to somebody. If you take the time to establish true and lasting connections by having a "You" mindset versus a "What's in it for me?" attitude I guarantee you that the lid to the 70% of amazing you are missing out on will begin to lift open. The result will not only shock you but often times put you in disbelief that amazing of that magnitude could ever find you. Before you know it, others will start calling you lucky!

THINGS TO REMEMBER

FIVE
Start Making Connections By Helping Others

CHAPTER 17

Own The Truck

hen I was a little boy, I used to get excited on Wednesday afternoons — garbage truck day. Not having a clear grasp of the power of hydraulics, I was convinced I could secretly hide something like a hunk of wood or piece of metal in our garbage that would render the compaction part of the truck useless. I became so enthralled with the challenge that after several weeks of trying, I decided that being a garbage man was my career goal. I still remember the day I came bounding into the house to tell my parents. They didn't even flinch when I told them my new passion. Instead they just said, "That's great! Just be sure you own the truck."

I had no idea what that meant back then, but as the years passed and I watched my folks work endless hours for other people so we could someday "own the truck" in our own newspaper business, I started to understand how my parents' minds worked. The path to true wealth (both financially as well as life) comes in either being your own boss or being in charge of your own destiny in some form or fashion. Again, this doesn't mean you can't make a great living as an employee, but I don't believe great wealth and freedom can be achieved without this critical ingredient.

Don't be alarmed if you are reading this and you realize the entrepreneurial spirit doesn't reside in you. Owning and running your own business isn't for everyone. In fact, it's not for most people! If you are satisfied being an employee for a company, good for you! But OWN your position! What

I mean is look at your company and your position as if you are the owner. Although in reality, you may be far down the pecking order in your company's hierarchy, it doesn't mean you have to act like it. Treat your position as if you are the CEO of it and act accordingly. Taking charge and assuming ownership of your role in the company will produce incredible rewards and tremendous growth. Why? Because, not very many employees do it. They are there to punch the clock and do what's minimally required. They are the ones leaving when the clock strikes five and always wondering why the company keeps passing them up for promotions.

It appears my folks were a rare breed when it came to raising my brother and me. Starting in middle school, we had "family meetings" where much of our family business was discussed. My folks explained our financial situation in great detail and what was happening in their business lives. They also discussed our family goals, which set the foundation for our financial future. Most importantly, both my brother and I were asked to participate in the sessions. These meetings came with one major rule that was never to be broken — like Las Vegas, what happened at our household meetings stayed in the house. Because my brother and I could both keep our mouths shut, the lessons continued, and over the years we climbed the learning curve. By the middle of high school, we had something that not many kids our age possessed — a solid understanding of taxes, profit and loss statements, and many of the critical aspects to owning and managing a business. When I graduated from college, I'll never forget my dad telling me that he had given my brother and me a ten year head start on our peers. That advice came with one caveat — it was up to us to stay ahead of them!

Why tell you this story? Because I find that very few parents take the time to sit their kids down and teach them what they've learned in the business world. Regardless if you're a CEO of a major corporation or working in a factory, you still understand certain basic principles about business and money that you can and should pass on to your children. Much like you can't expect a home built on sand to weather any kind of storm, you also can't expect your kids to emerge into adulthood without some solid financial foundation on which to build their lives.

Remember, no one is telling kids about things like taxes, something we all pay. How about what it takes to get hired, or better yet, what is required to keep from getting fired? The perils of credit card debt? I could keep going but you get the point. If you haven't started a family yet, keep learning so one day you can sit down with your kids and work with them. However, if you are a parent, start teaching! I bet your kids will have a greater interest than you thought. Stop fooling yourself into thinking that school will take care of this for you. School does an adequate job of teaching basics to kids, but it does a poor job of showing them what the real world truly looks like. Giving them a financial education is mandatory in order for them to succeed. The bottom line is only you can create an environment in your household that is conducive to learning about how things really work in the business world.

THINGS TO REMEMBER

SIX
Take Charge Of Your Own Destiny

SEVEN
Learn How Things Really Work In The
Business World

Finding a Job

It's not a surprise to hear about people being laid off from work, or worse yet, not being able to even find a company that will hire them. Because of this, many college graduates are taking up the spare bedroom in their folks' house. Have you ever wondered how some people seem to constantly struggle to find work, yet others seem to have offers coming at them left and right? Here's the trick — the successful ones consistently employ a couple of strategies that set them apart from the mob of people looking for work. The sad part is no one (until now) seems to be willing to share this knowledge, so you can begin thinking in ways you've never even dreamed of before.

There are two main aspects critical to landing a job: 1) discovering the job is available and 2) being invited in for a face-to-face interview. If you want to sit at home and read the classified ads in your local newspaper or drive around looking for help wanted signs in windows, be my guest. Many people have found out about jobs and made fine careers that way. But going this route in your job hunt is the long road to becoming employed and an even longer road to being financially successful. Why? Although you might get the job, there are going to be a ton of others reading the same ads and competing with you for the position. Do you know many high paying, cream-of-the-crop jobs are never advertised? Think about it. When's the last time you saw something other than an entry level job advertised? I don't think I've ever seen a sign in a window saying, "Now hiring managers and CEO's." That's because when a good job opens up, most companies are looking for a quick solution to fill the position with someone as good as or better than the person who just left. How do they usually do it? They tap into their network of business friends and find out who they might know that would be worth interviewing. By doing this, they separate the wheat from the chaff very quickly because someone they already trust knows this person and can give a reference that is both accurate and reliable. Doing so greatly increases the odds that the person will be a good hire. This is where the first two parts of this book come together to start showing amazing returns.

Many of my friends know I have a fairly expansive network of people in multiple professions, so they often come to me asking if I know if anyone has a job opening. No problem so far! They know me, appreciate that I have a lot of connections and are attempting to network to find the position no one knows about. Here's where the train goes off the tracks. I always follow up their question with, "So, what are you looking to do?" Most of the time their answer is, "Oh, I'll do anything." An answer like that is my favorite because no further action is required on my part. All I have to do is smile and forget about them when they walk away. Why? Because if you can't at least give me a rough idea what your interests are, then I know you haven't spent one waking minute trying to analyze how you could be a benefit to a company. When is the last time you saw someone advertise a job for "Anything?" That statement also shows me that you are unfocused. If you're that lost in your life, don't waste my time or anybody else's trying to help you find yourself. However, if someone comes to me and says, "Steve, I've studied construction science and would love to work for a builder specializing in commercial construction. Then I will jump at the chance to help them out.

Recently through my wife, I found out that one of our

operations was looking to fill a secretarial position. One of my wife's friends, Rebecca, sent her an e-mail recommending her friend, Janet, who was interviewing for the job. Rebecca went on to describe this terrific, upbeat person who would make a wonderful first impression on our customers and asked my wife to pass the message on to me. I gladly sent the message on to our manager of the operation, saying that Janet might be worth strong consideration. Guess what? She moved to the top of the resume pile and ended up getting the job. Normally, I wouldn't have even known we were hiring for that position, but because someone took the time to recommend a friend to a friend who shared the info with her husband (me) who forwarded the recommendation on to the decision-maker, Janet got the amazing job she wanted. Now that's making connections!

Networks are a double-edged sword that can make you or break you.

Think about this for a minute. Did the girl know me or anyone in the operation? No. But somewhere along the line she made a great impression on Rebecca who just happened to be friends with my wife. The recommendation didn't get her the job; it just gave her a free pass to the front of the line. Remember, your actions are constantly working for or against you, regardless of who you associate with. If Janet was in a bad mood the day Rebecca met her, do you think she would have sent the email? Do you think she would have gone to the front of the line? Networks are a double-edged sword that can make you or break you. It all depends on you. I've had many people call me over the years and tell me not to hire certain individuals because of what they witnessed on previous occasions. Does this job seeker ever know they just got submarined? Never. But they will always wonder why they never seem to catch a break.

It's not just the unemployed people utilizing a network, plenty of business people are as well. One of the first things we do when we have an upper level position come open in our company is send out an e-mail to about twenty of my business friends explaining the position and asking them if they know of someone capable of doing the job. Most of the time, I begin my job search with at least three names of very qualified candidates who are looking to change jobs or have been let go due to issues out of their control.

Another strategy that seems to be a forgotten art in the world of job hunting is using the "Everyone's Favorite Subject" rule I talked about in the previous section. I lecture college students about career fairs that come to colleges about twice a year. A career fair is an event where multiple businesses come in to show off their company and to collect resumes for current or potential job openings. I ask the students if they attend and most reluctantly raise their hands. They seem relieved when I tell them the *way* they are going about it is completely wrong. They appear relieved because they *know* it's a waste of time but they don't know how to change the situation into a productive one.

The goal (whether you're at a career fair or hunting for a new job) is to have your resume be at the top of the pile in order to give you a chance for a face-to-face with the interviewer. I tell the students to identify about five companies they would like to work for and do some research on them before attending the job fair. With some basic knowledge in hand, the candidate should focus on interviewing the people representing the company. Why? Because they hold the real key to what the company is looking for in an employee. More importantly, they likely know what the interviewer back at headquarters is like, and it's a huge bonus if the applicant can find out what the interviewers passions are prior to the interview.

Remember, at the end of a career fair the businesses gather up their belongings (and a huge pile of resumes) and haul it all back to the office. I assure you that by the time they start the boring job of reviewing resumes, they can't remember any one person's face, character or personality. This is where the job hunter who came with a different mindset changes the game. While their friends were passing out resumes like crazy, they were gathering information about the company's needs, as well as some personal tidbits about the interviewer. While the attendees are back home hoping and praying someone reads their resume, the smart prospector is sitting down writing out a handwritten note to the interviewer (remember, you should know his/her name by now) and include a small gift, preferably in an area of their outside interest, e.g. a sleeve of golf balls if you discovered they were a golfer. If you've done your homework correctly, your resume will be placed on the top of the pile and an interview will likely be granted, if for nothing else than to express their appreciation for the gift.

Recently I saw on the local news that a big industry was hiring for 100 entry-level positions. About a thousand people stood in line since five that morning hoping to land an interview. Watching as the camera panned back and forth along the long line of people, I couldn't help but shake my head. I wondered how many of them ever thought about what they could do to differentiate themselves from the hundreds of others standing alongside of them. I doubt many, if any, did. I can guess what would have happened if one had taken the time to learn about the company and people doing the interviewing. Although they might not have landed the job, they sure would have stood out among all the other warm bodies waiting in line.

THINGS TO REMEMBER

EIGHT
Differentiate Yourself From The Crowd

CHAPTER 19

Getting Hired

So now you've been invited in for an interview, putting you one step ahead of your peers. The trick to getting a leg up in being the chosen one is in knowing everything about the company. I wouldn't hesitate to call a few people in the company just to chat them up and ask them what the company likes to see in its new hires. Remember, NO ONE asks employees stuff like that, and they usually are more than willing to express their wisdom to you. By the way, the best person to become friends with is the interviewer's administrative assistant. Most people don't realize the power many assistants have. Many times, the assistant is the gatekeeper to the whole show. Make her mad — or worse — treat her like she is not important, and you might as well fall on the knife yourself.

Speaking of administrative assistants, similar powers reside with a person working the front counter of a retail store. Because of this, I've included a side note for all the sales people out there. Do you want to know a quick way into the owner's office? Just walk in the store and ask the person (I don't care if they are a teenager) working the register if they are the manager or owner. Ninety-nine percent of the time they aren't, but they are so impressed with the fact that you *thought* they were that they will be more than happy to personally bring you to the right person! Often times, I notice they will stand up straighter and immediately smile with pride just because you thought of them in such a manner! Unfortunately, the reverse is true as well. I'm ashamed to admit that there have been a few times in my sales career that I've walked into a store and, convinced the person at the counter was just an hourly worker, asked them if I could talk to the manager. When the person responds with "I'm the manager." I kick myself and know it's strike one, two and three...I'm out!

Figuring out what the proper attire is for the interview should be one of the first questions asked, along with specific directions to where the interview will be held. Other questions should include what the work environment is like, what to expect in the interview, whether or not the company is growing, do they enjoy working there, etc. Make sure you arrive early (I simply won't hire someone who is late to an interview) and don't be afraid to open up and once again, chat with some of the folks in the office. Remember, if you get the job these people are going to have to work with you the majority of every day. If they like you from the onset, often times they will put a word in for you without you even having to ask.

Many times a job is awarded to the person the interviewer likes the most, not the most qualified.

Your head should be on a swivel the moment you walk into the interviewer's office. Why? Although they are going to be asking you serious questions, they are still normal people just like you and me. What do you think they'd rather talk about, your strengths and weaknesses or what they are passionate about? If you were to walk into my office, you'd have to be blind not to realize my passions lie in two areas — aviation and my family. It's obvious because virtually every picture is either of an airplane or something related to my wife and kids. I don't care if I'm having the busiest day of my life, if you walk in and ask me about flying or my family, I will immediately have some extra time to talk to you about it. Not only do I like to talk about it (I call it my happy place), but I appreciate you for asking. Remarkably, over half the people who walk into my office never inquire about it. If someone I'm interviewing starts showing true curiosity towards me and my passions, then they are already ahead of the competition because I will naturally appreciate them for their interest. Again, do not confuse this with sucking up and asking about it just for the sake of asking. That is far worse than not asking at all! If you aren't truly curious to learn, then please save you and the interviewer time — you'll never have a prayer of being hired because the interviewer will see right through you.

Here's something else most people don't realize — many times a job is awarded to the person the interviewer *likes* the most, not the most qualified. A prospect might have a lot of talent, but if he or she is a jerk or has no interpersonal skills, no one is going to look forward to dealing with that person for eight hours every day. I have a friend who is very familiar with the aerospace industry where just about everyone working in that field is super smart with multiple high level college degrees — super geeks if you will. He told me everyone who applies for an open position always has the academic credentials to succeed in the job. So who ends up getting the job offer? The person who can engage people well and has the ability to fit in with the rest of the office staff. In short, the person they *like* the best!

Even if you're not in someone's office to be interviewed, the technique of engaging in small talk can do wonders for your profit margins. When I was a salesperson, I would routinely walk into people's offices trying to convince them why they should be buying advertising from me. Talking about their passion, regardless of what it was, always got me off on the right foot with them. One day it helped me make a quarter million dollars!

My newspaper had a major advertiser whose advertising agreement was up for renewal and there was some serious doubt if they would renew. I didn't want to blame anyone but myself if this went poorly, so I went personally to the corporate office to convince the customer that a new agreement would be a positive for all parties. Trust me, a quarter million dollar contract was no small agreement and I really couldn't afford to lose the business.

I realized I had a serious problem when I walked into the regional vice president's office and saw the walls of his office were completely bare. Worse, there was only a notepad and pen on his desk. No pictures, no art, nothing! As we sat there for a few minutes making small talk, I could almost see the dollar bills and my agreement going out the window. Then I asked the golden question: "What do you like to do when you're not working?" His facial expression completely changed (he went to his happy place) and he told me quite proudly — wait for it — that he likes to collect G.I. Joe action figures. Now I thought I was ready for anything he was going to say, but I never expected a grown man who was V.P. of a major corporation to openly express his love for G.I. Joes. I knew if I busted out laughing the joke was going to be on me, so I held it together and decided it was time for me to learn all I could about G.I. Joes. The meeting (interview) was easy sailing from there. I left with some new-found knowledge about G.I. Joes, and he left thrilled he got to talk about them. I didn't ask for the order because I had a better idea that I felt would raise my success rate from 80% to 100%.

I went back home and wrote him a thank you letter for taking the time to meet me, and I enclosed a $75.00 collector G.I. Joe. On top of the whole package was a fresh new contract just waiting for his signature. Needless to say, he was thrilled with the gift and couldn't sign the agreement fast enough. Do you think any other reps figured that out? I doubt it.

But I do know this — for a small investment of time and a meaningful gift, I made a friend and reaped a $250,000 return — all because I asked questions and listened. So, whether you're selling a product or selling yourself during an interview, the point is to ask questions. Then, listen and learn. You never know what you will discover that allows you to make an amazing connection that changes your life.

Now, back to your interview! Let's assume you've executed all the above strategies correctly, and the first interview went well. You even had a chance to interview the interviewer a little bit, and everyone walked away happy. You now have a couple of choices to make. You can sit back and hope you're the top candidate, or you can take control of the situation and make yourself the top candidate. "That's impossible," you say. Not really. Here's why...

Much like in sales, the interviewer needs to find something that separates you from the other top candidates (salespeople call it a close). I don't care how long and detailed the interview is, you and the other interviewees are still unknown, which makes it a crap shoot for the company to pick the right person. This is where you supply the difference. Before you leave the interview, make a guarantee I assure you they have never heard before. Tell them that you want to be part of the company bad enough that you're willing to make them a deal. You will work for the company for FREE up to three months with the following caveat. They agree that if you bust your rear and do an excellent job they will grant you a permanent position with the company at the agreed upon salary. You also tell them that if you don't do a satisfactory job, they can tell you to hit the door (I would offer to sign something that releases them from liability as well) and not look back. I realize this might sound radical, but I have seen it work for many people. It really makes you stand light years ahead of other job seekers.

This strategy comes with one word of caution — you must want this job with all your heart and soul (if not, don't do this). Now think about this for a minute. You've just offered the company a risk-free look at you. If you do the job right they win, and if you don't, they can release you without problems coming back to haunt them. You've now turned an unknown and potentially risky hire into a guaranteed win for the company. It's an offer that is VERY hard for an interviewer to say "no" to. If you're thinking, "What about me? I have all the risk." Welcome to the business world! But remember this, you're most likely going to spend at least three months searching for a job (for free) so proving yourself with a potential positive outcome shouldn't be a problem if you're willing to bust your butt. If you're not willing to work hard, then you probably aren't the right person for the job anyway. Consider it simply saving you and the company a lot of money and time.

THINGS TO REMEMBER

NINE
Invest In Others and Reap The Rewards

TEN
People Do Amazing Things When They Like You

CHAPTER 20

.

Which Side Are You On?

bet you know someone who's been fired recently. I see it happen to people I know almost on a continual basis. With the economy being so uncertain, it has become commonplace to hear about people losing their jobs and the hardships they suffer because of it. A few nights ago, I got a call from a schoolteacher friend who had just received word that he was out of a job in thirty days. No reasons, no severance pay, just out! He had twelve hard years into teaching at the school. In the end, there are only so many ways to slice the pie and someone higher up decided he wasn't a necessary ingredient. Now he's calling people like me looking for work. I advised him to stop and reconsider which part of a business he wants to participate in. I explained that there is a certain group of individuals who go to work everyday extremely confident their company would most likely close down before firing them. Why? Because they are too important to the company.

....
The first employees to go when things get bad are the ones on the expense side of the business.
....

So the million dollar question is how do you know if you're safe or not? Here it is — the first employees to go when things get bad are the ones on the expense side of the business. Huh? Almost every business has people working on two distinct sides of the income statement. Some people work on the side associated with bringing money into the company (revenue) and some are associated with doing jobs that, while necessary, cost the company money (expense) in things like salary. Here is a simple economics problem for you. If business slows and layoffs are required, which employees do you think your company is going to let go? The ones *making* the company money or the ones *costing* it money? I guarantee you it's the people on the expense side of the business.

I know people who go to work every day wondering if this is the day they get fired. They live a life so stressed it's hard to imagine how anything in their life can be good. What they don't ever consider is *why* they are worried. It's easy to fantasize that the company would never fire someone like you because you are so loyal, hard working and capable, but in the end, the thing that usually matters to most companies is the profit margin. Most businesses simply can't afford to fire someone who's bringing in revenue to the company, yet the most loyal expense worker will be let go without a second thought. If this offends you, too bad, because this is how things really go down in the back rooms of corporate America. I'm telling you this because no one else is! I encourage you to immediately examine where you fall in the big scheme of things. If you're not already a revenue employee then you better find a way to bring additional revenues to your company...and fast! If you're not willing to make that change, then feel free to continue living a stressful life because I can assure you that you'll be one of the first to go in hard times, despite your good looks and seemingly irreplaceable qualities.

Here is a real world example: In a newspaper you have a variety of departments and many people working to produce the paper. The advertising sales reps are responsible for bringing in the majority of the revenue while the reporters are tasked with writing most of the news. When times get tight and cuts are needed, which one do you think is the first to go? You guessed it, it's the reporter. Why? Because although a reporter is very important to a newspaper, the revenue is critically important. A newspaper can use the wire service (news provided by national companies) or temporarily give their audience less news, but they can't afford to fire the sales rep because they would lose the thousands of dollars the rep was bringing in from their efforts. Because of this, when hard decisions need to be made, the revenue person is typically in a very safe position.

The moral of the story is this — be on the revenue side of business, if possible. If you can't, then read the next chapter.

THINGS TO REMEMBER

ELEVEN
Be On The Revenue Side Of The Business

CHAPTER 21

Results, Results, Results

What happens if you discover you're not a revenue person in your company and don't have any idea how to bring in additional revenues? What do you do? Although it's not quite as effective as being a revenuer, there's another secret that seems incredibly obvious but most people don't do it. Just get results! I don't care what profession you're in. If you are the person who simply gets things done, then you instantly become someone who is not only hard to fire but even harder to replace. Why? Because most people want to do as little as possible and blame anyone they can for their failures.

On the other hand, we all know people who jump on a task, and all you have to do is get out of their way. If that doesn't have value then I don't know what does! Look around your office or think about your friends. How many of them really step up and take the lead to push projects through? Not many. So if you are stuck on the non-revenue side of the business but don't want to worry about your future, be sure you become the go-to person in your company. I've seen some people who are absolute jerks keep their jobs while the fun, friendly employees are packing up their belongings and being escorted out the door. Why? Even though the person might be a jerk, they are able to produce results for the company. At the end of the day, and especially in tough times, that's what matters most to companies.

For example, my friend Todd is a lead engineer in one of the world's largest electrical companies. Because he's an engineer, he isn't on the revenue side of the business and knows it. But Todd makes up for it by being the guy that gets things done and pulls projects through to completion. Without him, he's confident that the company's profits would be negatively impacted because they couldn't get most of their projects to market in a timely manner. Here's where he separates himself. While all of the other engineers are having meeting after meeting, Todd is pushing the project through and seeing direct results (and profits) from his actions. Does this make him important? You bet! Remarkably, his company has been having layoffs and everyone is worried about their future…everyone but Todd. He goes to work every day knowing his job will be there, and he would be one of the last ones to go in any cutback.

Being someone who gets things done also has a way of accelerating your move up the company hierarchy. People who step up and just do it always understand that excuses for failure aren't acceptable and that stress is a given. They learned a long time ago that in order for success to knock on your door, you must be willing to accept responsibility for your actions.

Just get results!

Have you ever watched the TV show "Celebrity Apprentice?" Periodically, I'll waste an hour of my life watching it just to see how famous celebrities handle real world tasks. If you've seen the show, you know the result is often disastrous. That's not what annoys me. What annoys me is their complete and utter refusal to take responsibility for their own actions. The celebrities are always broken into teams to compete against each other. Each team always has a designated leader charged with taking the team to victory. Every episode ends with the losing team being pulled into the boardroom to face Donald Trump. He asks them a series of pointed questions, trying to figure out who was the weakest link, so he can say his famous line, "You're fired!"

I believe the public's respect and admiration would soar if just once someone said, "Blame me and no one else." I think it would be a great example for viewers to start realizing that taking responsibility for your actions has specific results. I know that I would hesitate to fire someone if they assumed responsibility for a failure — that's just part of the learning process. The trick is not to repeat the same mistakes over and over. That's called stupidity and is a totally different issue!

Finally, I don't care what profession you are in, get results and you will have much greater job security and most likely be someone who moves up in your organization.

THINGS TO REMEMBER

TWELVE
Get Results To Increase Job Security

Part III • It Depends on You!

CHAPTER 22

Honey, I'm Home!

Now it's time to talk about marriage. Say what? What does marriage have to do with being successful in business? A lot more than you think! There's an old quote, "Be careful who you choose for your lifelong mate, because they will bring you 95% of your happiness or 95% of your misery." That pretty much says it all. But I want to add one more thing — the right or wrong spouse can also have a major impact on whether or not you are successful in business.

In my career as a business owner and entrepreneur, I have had days that were so bad it's hard to describe. Throughout all the turmoil, one thing has remained constant. I know when the day is done and I walk in the door of my home, my wife will be thrilled to see me and will always have a smile on her face. As bad as the day was, I *know* that it won't continue when I get home.

Unfortunately, I have friends who dread going home, regardless of how bad their day was. They know that there will be more stress and fighting going on the minute they walk in. The result is just a continuation of the problems and stress they just spent eight or more hours dealing with. So what do they do? They delay going home as long as possible. They work late hours, play golf, go to the bar, take company trips or worse, they cheat on their spouse. Who suffers? Everyone! I guarantee you the person's job performance is not all it could be when they are dealing with constant problems at home. Does this lead to success? No. When someone isn't happy both at work and home, it's hard to keep the focus and business mindset required for success to show up in your life.

When I'm speaking to young, single audiences I stress the importance of the lifelong impact the right or wrong spouse can have on your business career. I recount a conversation I had with a friend of mine back in my single days to as many of these people as possible in the hopes they learn from it. I had been dating a girl for over a year and the natural progression of things seemed to be marriage. She voiced several times she hoped we would tie the knot somewhere in our near future. However, there was one major problem. Although I believed I loved her, my gut kept telling me that being with her for the *rest of my life* wouldn't be the right thing.

One night I was sitting in a car talking to one of my friends, Chuck, about marriage. He was about fifteen years older than me, the pastor of my church and happily married with several kids, so I figured he was a good person to bounce these feelings off of. I explained my current relationship and then asked him what turned out to be one of the most important questions in my life. I said, "Chuck, how do you know when you've met the right girl?" His answer was like a clap of thunder! He said, "Steve, if you're asking, she's not the one." You know what? He was right. We broke up and a few years later I met the girl who would become my wife. Here's the kicker — when I asked her to marry me I knew with all of my heart she was the person I wanted to share the rest of my life with. The question never even came up. Fifteen years later I can't imagine not having her as my personal confidant. She is my best friend and our talks are something I always enjoy. She also does a wonderful job of helping me keep my head screwed on straight.

If you're single, I hope you take the time to make sure you're choosing the right spouse for the right reasons. Obviously, people aren't doing so well at picking the right spouse since the divorce rate is over 50%. When I was single, I knew I was ignorant about marriage so I did what most people don't — I asked questions about it. Whenever I was afforded the opportunity, I would ask married guys for any tips about marriage. Most of the time I was told (only half joking) not to do it. Then they would rattle off a list of negative things about their marriage as well as their wife. I often walked away wishing I could tell them how bad they sounded. I wanted to say, "It sounds like you chose poorly." I bet many of these guys were better golfers than husbands or fathers.

....
If you don't have a team at home then it's hard to really have your suit of armor on when you go off to work
....

If you are reading this and are one of the unhappy people I mentioned above, all I can say is do whatever it takes to make the situation better. I'm not a marriage counselor, but many times just communicating with each other and re-connecting with what brought you together in the first place can do a lot of good. Stop asking "WIFM" (what's in it for me) and start asking what you can do for your spouse. If you can help each other through the problems you're dealing with, find some common goals and then be willing to pitch in and help each other through it, I think things will only get better.

However you improve your current situation, know that it's integral to your success or failure in the world of business. The bottom line is if you don't have a team at home then it's hard to really have your suit of armor on when you go off to work. It's also virtually impossible to teach your kids anything about life, love and business if you and your spouse are constantly bickering. It's also extremely difficult to find amazing things in your life when there is constant tension at home.

So, choose wisely, keep the communication open and work as a team to create an amazing life at home and in the business world.

THINGS TO REMEMBER

THIRTEEN
Choose An Amazing Spouse and Keep the
Communication Open

FOURTEEN
Work As A Team To Create An Amazing Life

IN A NUTSHELL
14 Ways To Succeed In the Business World

ONE
Choices Determine Your Destiny

TWO
Desire Wins Every Time

THREE
People Choose You When You Stand Out

FOUR
Great Communication Creates Great Wealth
In All Areas Of Your Life

FIVE
Start Making Connections By Helping Others

SIX
Take Charge Of Your Own Destiny

SEVEN
Learn How Things Really Work In The Business World

(continued)

IN A NUTSHELL
14 Ways To Succeed In the Business World (continued)

EIGHT
Differentiate Yourself From The Crowd

NINE
Invest In Others and Reap The Rewards

TEN
People Do Amazing Things When They Like You

ELEVEN
Be On The Revenue Side Of The Business

TWELVE
Get Results To Increase Job Security

THIRTEEN
Choose An Amazing Spouse and Keep
the Communication Open

FOURTEEN
Work As A Team To Create An Amazing Life

THE FINAL TEST

So there it is! Now ask yourself the question, "Who's in charge of you?" Once you answer that, it changes everything.

Remember, it's not about you! But…it starts with you, and it depends on you. I hope you use the strategies shared in this book as a jumping off point to begin your journey to an amazing life filled with adventure, happiness and success. If you challenge yourself, show genuine interest in others and differentiate yourself in the business world, you will be surprised, if not shocked, at how fast things change for you and the amount of success you can achieve.

I tell my kids all too frequently (they even roll their eyes many times), "If it were easy, everyone would do it." So you need to decide whether or not you're up to the challenge. If I've done what I hoped, then I've hit a few nerves throughout these chapters. Many times, all it takes is someone or something making you aware of weaknesses in your life or the realities in life to elicit a change.

When you break it down, it really isn't that hard, as long as you're willing to take off your rose-colored glasses and see things for what they are. Only then can you have the ability to make the appropriate changes. One of my favorite quotes is: "Everyone is self made — only the successful admit it." It speaks to virtually everything I have talked about and says in one sentence all that I have tried to teach throughout this entire book. Take responsibility for your life and all that is going on in it and start changing it from average to amazing.

Remember, nothing happens at once. Almost anyone who is successful has become so through a series of small steps that eventually lead to something great. The trick is to be *willing* to start taking those steps. I'll tell you one last secret — many times the most amazing experiences come from the journey... not the destination.

Let me leave you with this. Many times after I give a speech on how to transform your life from average to amazing, I have audience members wanting to spend more time with me in the hopes of elevating their life to a higher level. I always make time for them and find that as we talk, they oftentimes believe that I have the power to inject amazing straight into them with my insights, experience and knowledge. What they don't realize is, in the end, I don't have the power to make their life amazing. Only they do.

Ultimately, I tell them that if they want to HAVE amazing lives ... then BE amazing people!

And that's my final thought for you! When it's all said and done, it's really a decision you have to make. You have to get uncomfortable with where you are, want more and go for it!

The time is now! Go grab some amazing!

EPILOGUE

Although this isn't a religious book, I don't think I would be showing all of my cards if I didn't include a section on my belief in the importance of having faith in God.

I'm not here to sway your religious beliefs; all I know is that I believe for you to live an amazing life (however you define amazing) you must have a belief that there is a higher power at work in your life. Many times people disguise this belief by saying they believe in fate or that things happen in their lives for a reason. I find it easier to simply say that I believe in God and that, ultimately, he is at the controls of everything in my life. Again, I'm not here to sway you toward one religion or another, I just believe it's important to realize that as much as you *think* what you're doing brings wonderful things into your life, there is a higher power at work doing much more.

Personally, I never had much (if any) understanding of the Bible or what a life of faith could do for someone. When a conversation about the Bible would come up, I became the quietest person in the room. Don't get me wrong! I *wanted* to be part of the conversation, but I was too ignorant about the Bible to offer anything relevant. Throughout the years, I attended quite a few churches and always found myself doing the same thing during every sermon — sitting there bored out of my mind, checking my watch to see how long we had until it was over. Because I had mentally checked out, I always left just as ignorant about the Bible and its meaning as I had come. I often amused myself by sitting there wondering what would happen if I stood up during one of those boring sermons and yelled "Stop!" and asked anyone if they could repeat the last sentence the pastor had just spoken. I might be wrong, but I don't think many people could have repeated it. I think most of the congregation was sitting there in a fog, just like me.

Why this story? Because like many things in life, my wife and I got tired of going to church just for the sake of saying we did. So we changed it! We started visiting churches to find one that could teach us something and make it worth our while to get up on Sunday and go. Once again, our network of friends came through for us. A family down the street from us heard we were shopping around and suggested we try a new church in the neighboring city. We had an open mind and nothing to lose, so we decided to jump in the car one Sunday and check them out.

Amazingly, we found a church that conducted itself in a completely new way. They had a great band that could sing in tune (a whole new concept for me), and more importantly, a preacher who spoke a message in such a way you were completely locked on to what he said. Best of all, his excellent speaking style — coupled with his use of examples — helped you understand the meaning of every Bible passage he talked about. I'm willing to bet that if I yelled "Stop!" at this church, 95% of the people would easily be able to repeat what he'd just said. Not surprisingly, it's one of the fastest growing churches in the country (I guess it wasn't just me in the fog). Through attending and becoming friends with the pastor and staff, I have some remarkable mentors when it comes to learning about the Bible and its meaning. This has led to another benefit of a good network of friends — the people I know at this church are some of my closest friends and are just good down to the core. Being around them and their positive energy helps me fill up my tank in regards to my outlook on life.

We often hear some of our friends complain about their church and the gossip and arguing going on in it. On several occasions, we have asked these people to come take a look at something different — not join our church — just experience it. Unfortunately, most of the time we are NOT appreciated for our concern. Although they dread going to church on Sunday, they still won't consider something new. It is a lot easier for them to *talk* about the problem rather than *fix* it. The really sad part is that most of the time I think it's because they fear repercussions from their friends who are miserable with them. I can't help but wonder what else in their life needs changing but remains on the same dead end road because they fear they might be viewed poorly by their friends.

My pastor shared an excellent example one day that really brought things into focus for me. He asked if we ever noticed that every game of Monopoly always ends the same way. You always pick up the board and slide all the accumulated pieces back into the box. His point was the same for life. All of our possessions really don't matter in the end. When you die, they all get slid back into the box. He reminded us that eternity is a lot longer than the few years we spend on earth. Living your life with that in mind can bring rewards to you well beyond your years here. For me, being a Christian has enabled me to know in good times and bad, God is there watching my family and making sure that in the end, no matter what happens, everything will work out.

ACKNOWLEDGEMENTS

I hate to admit it, but in the hundreds of books I've read I have rarely taken the time to read the acknowledgment page where the author thanks all the people who helped him write their book.

I hope you take an extra minute to read this one! Like the saying, "It takes a village to raise a child," the same could be said for a book.

Three years ago I would have thought you were off your rocker if you told me I would write a book that could impact and change lives around the world. One thing I know for sure — although you will never cross paths with many of the people I'm about to mention — the quality of people surrounding you and pushing you to higher levels can truly make the impossible suddenly become very possible.

This whole journey started years ago when my wife would periodically tell me, "You should write a book." My immediate answer would always be, "About what?" A book seemed like something others do and I never really imagined it would be something I could do.

Soon thereafter, through a series of very unusual circumstances, I found myself invited to speak in Dave Wyman's entrepreneurship class at Clemson University. My first presentation went well and turned into another and another. The fateful day came after one of my presentations when Dave pulled me aside and asked me if I had ever seriously considered writing a book. I guess it took a second person to believe in me enough to push me over the edge and start the process. Bottom line, this book would have never happened without Dave. For that, I am eternally grateful. Not only did he get me started, but he stayed with me throughout the whole process, gently nudging me in the direction I needed to go. To this day I call him my personal "Yoda" because he never *tells* me what to do. He simply poses a question that is too pointed to ignore.

Through the months of writing I also turned to Ed and Betsy Byars for additional input and motivation. I talk about Ed and Betsy in the book, so here I will simply say thanks for taking the time to read the book repeatedly and give me invaluable feedback.

Another thanks is due to Professor Elaine Worzala for offering up not only her own wisdom, but also her class of forty very bright graduate students. She assigned them to read and review my book. If you don't think colleges are producing some remarkable people, you should see the reviews. They were some of the most well-written, comprehensive reviews any author could hope for.

To this day, I'm not sure which is harder...writing a book or the endless edits required to polish it into its final form! I'm a pretty good writer, but I was soon humbled and grateful when people with true talent edited my copy.

Fortunately, the editing process became much easier because of my incredible network of friends. They simply came through for me in spades. People like Casey Frid, Melinda Connally, Raye Harville, Doug and Cindy Grant, Karla McCollum, Scott Hartzell, Rob Green, Scott Vick, Judith and Mark McKnew, Kelly Durham, Jonathan Stano, Keith McGregor, Bill and Suzanne Swedberg, Blake and Lisa Joplin, Shane Duffy, Josh Olson and Melissa Bradley, all spent hours reading, correcting and suggesting different viewpoints for me to take. On top of that, they did this simply because I asked. That alone speaks volumes. I assure you that without each of their specific skill sets, this book would only be half of what it is. Thank you all from the bottom of my heart.

Through all of this, my wife patiently watched me spend endless hours typing away. She always encouraged me and was willing to stop anything she was doing in order to read chapters or just let me bounce ideas off her. She is one of the happiest and most giving people I know, and I thank God every day I found her for my lifelong mate.

I also want to thank my brother Jerry for picking up the slack while I was absorbed in this project. We run a fairly large company, and when I was hiding to write my book, there were many times he had to catch some things falling through the cracks caused by my absence. Thanks, bro!

I have talked to several people who have written a manuscript but never found the time to actually publish it. Now I know why. Without people like Rhonda Olson and Kristi Keenan I don't think I would have had the ability to push this over the finish line. They did an amazing job of tying up all the loose ends from the final polish editing to copyright to design and layout. The result of their work can be described like the feeling you have when you've been driving down a gravel road for miles, and suddenly it turns into a smooth paved one. They were the pavement for my gravel road and I thank you so much.

Finally to anyone who has a dream of someday writing their own book. All I can say is that if I can do it so can you! Like the rest of this book will show you, the potential for amazing resides inside of you just waiting to be tapped. Start taking small steps, and before you know it, your dream will become reality.

Now, go be amazing!

ABOUT THE AUTHOR

 Steve Edwards, a prominent businessman, professional speaker and author, has both a unique ability and a passion for inspiring people to lead amazing lives, and that drive carries over into everything he does.

Steve is an expert in making real and lasting relationships and has the innate ability to read people and discern what they are searching for in life and in business. His extensive media sales background has helped him hone the art of crafting and delivering an effective message, a skill he has used to coach salespeople, market his own invention, increase his company's holdings and personally connect with audiences from all walks of life.

Committed to living an amazing life, Steve invests his time and energy in growing his businesses, spending time with his family, developing his network of relationships and maintaining a fit and healthy lifestyle. Passionate about flying, with 25 years of experience, Steve enjoys flying his company airplane for various business ventures as well as to benefit a multitude of charitable organizations.

Through his newest company, The Amazing Factor, Steve inspires people to take responsibility for their own actions and take the steps necessary to bring success into their lives. His book, "Who's In Charge Of You? Answer That & Change Everything," serves as a companion to his inspirational speaking engagements and a way to help his audiences move forward with their own amazing lives.

Whether he is playing with his kids, coaching a young college student, mentoring a friend or business associate or flying a sick patient cross country, Steve is driven by his motto. "If you want to HAVE an amazing life, then BE an amazing person."

Steve resides in Clemson, South Carolina, with his wife, Karen, and children, Blake and Jenna.

Sales
Relationships
Health
Business
Life
Got Questions?
Networking
Career
Leadership
Money
Get Answers With Attitude!
Join the conversation at...
www.AskSteveEdwards.com

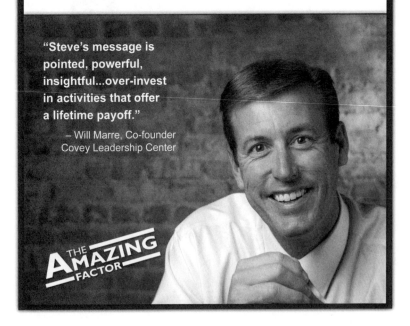